SHANGHAI

THE ARCHITECTURE OF CHINA'S GREAT URBAN CENTER

Jay Pridmore

Abrams, New York

CONTENTS

Page 1: Jin Mao Tower
Pages 2–3: Pudong
Page 4: Shanghai Grand Theater (foreground) and Tomorrow Square
Left: Tai chi on the Bund

INTRODUCTION TO SHANGHAI

SHANGHAI'S ARCHITECTURE at the turn of the millennium was overwhelming. Three thousand skyscrapers of more than thirty stories had been built since 1992. Perhaps even more stupefying than the amount of construction was the architectural audacity that had imbued the city with ostentatious colors and flamboyant forms. The exuberance and contradictions reshaping Shanghai practically cried out for a crime novelist, an expert in sifting for the telling detail, to explain. Indeed, Qiu Xiaolong, a Shanghai-born writer residing in the United States, specializes in exploring the city's tumultuous transformation through the device of the detective genre.

Qiu's 2002 book, *A Loyal Character Dancer*, set in the mid-1990s, captures a China in rapid transition, with all the tensions and complexity inherent in a communist society's shift toward capitalism. In it, police detective Chen Cao is investigating a cabal of gangsters and is about to connect the criminals to high government officials. Though Chen had little time for daydreaming, one morning on the Bund, Shanghai's famous riverfront, he stopped to listen to the chiming from the old Custom House's clock tower. Built in 1928, it was once a symbol of British dominance; it was even modeled after London's Big Ben. But the building's meaning had changed over the years. By the 1960s and the onset of Mao Zedong's Cultural Revolution, its bells played "The East Is Red," the Chinese Communist anthem. Now, with China once again cultivating business, the clock announced the beginning of the workday with a simple chime.

"Time flowed away like water," Chen thought. The detective looked across the Huangpu River at Shanghai's vast new commercial district, Pudong. Its postmodern convention center, built in 1994 and flanked by massive globes, "stood like a monster . . . slouching against the first gray of the morning." Shanghai "had been changing, though [Chen] did not like some of the changes. . . . So, too, had Chen changed, from a penniless student to a prominent police inspector."

Shanghai, China's largest city and greatest trading center, was transforming architecturally and in just about every other way. On the boulevard that ran along the Bund, dozens of palatial buildings to either side of the Custom House were being renovated and new stores were freshly stocked with luxury goods. Old neighborhoods were being swept away to make room for soaring office towers. Fashionable restaurants were cropping up across from outdoor market stalls heaped with produce, cages of live poultry, and icy bins of seafood. Pudong's hulking convention center was part of a rising skyline that evoked the one Fritz Lang envisioned in his futuristic 1927 film *Metropolis*.

Custom House
PALMER AND TURNER, 1928
This was the last of three buildings on this site along the Bund that served as the trading port's custom house. The Custom House symbolized the colonial administration, not only because the British largely controlled imports but also because the large public clock reflected concepts of time and punctuality unfamiliar in China prior to the Europeans' arrival.

Pudong
Across the Huangpu River from the Bund, Pudong was the hub of the building surge that began in the 1990s. As each developer sought to outdo the other, Pudong became famous for its otherworldly skyline, pierced by the Oriental Pearl tower and anchored by the convention center wedged between two globes.

**Shanghai International
Convention Center**
NIKKEN SEKKEI WITH ARCHITECTURAL DESIGN
INSTITUTE OF ZHEJIANG PROVINCE, 1994
The convention center, a postmodern
design by the Japanese firm Nikken
Sekkei, was built early in the Pudong
building boom. With Roman arches
and glass globes, the architects
meant to address the past and the
future in equal measure.

Some find the city's speeded-up modernization exhilarating, others distress-
ing. Architecture critic Christopher Hawthorne, a frequent visitor, wrote of his
own mixed reaction in the *Los Angeles Times* in 2005. Upon arriving in Shanghai,
he would routinely drop his bags at the hotel and "head directly for one of the
rooftop bars and restaurants lining the Bund . . . the best place from which to as-
sess Shanghai's sometimes daring, sometimes schizophrenic attempts to balance
Chinese urbanism and outside influence."

He's probably right that it doesn't hurt to have a drink in hand when drawing
your eye across the spectacle of the skyline and taking in its glittering contradictions. For example, the restored, prosperous Bund expresses the glamour of the
new Shanghai even as it echoes the city's decadent past. Across the river, Pudong's
abrupt metamorphosis from farmland to financial capital bears witness to the
ability of the Chinese, with help from planeloads of American and European
architects, to shake off the Cultural Revolution and promote an unprecedented
building boom. Between 1992 and 2002 real estate investment in Shanghai rock-
eted from $160 million to $9.2 billion.

One might well ask if the new China's rampant capitalism and exuberant
growth have come at too high a price economically, socially, and aesthetically.
(Few places in the world have so many buildings that provoke wonder about
what the architects might have been thinking.) The rush to develop reveals

Shanghai's impatience to meet its presumed future as China's epicenter without entirely coming to terms with its past. For much of the nineteenth and twentieth centuries Shanghai precariously balanced countless incongruities—including European traders, Nationalists, pitiless gangsters, Communists, jazz, opium, and a *Chinese* stock market dating to the 1920s. Today everything in Shanghai has changed except its fragile equilibrium.

THE CITY'S POSITION near the mouth of the Yangtze River, which almost bisects China, made it a flourishing trading center coveted throughout its history by both ferocious antagonists and unlikely allies. Instead of the regular grid of most other Chinese cities, Shanghai's streets corresponded roughly to the curve of the Huangpu River, a wide tributary of the Yangtze, and creeks running through the city. The original town center, small parts of which survive, was encircled by a city wall built in the 1500s, when Japanese and Chinese pirates found the environs an easy mark for invasion and looting. Within the walls, the city was laid out in a tight network of *hutongs*, courtyard buildings typical of Chinese cities. Despite its defenses, bustling old Shanghai was hardly insular: It was designed for trade with outsiders, not protection from them. The city's plazas were larger, its markets more active than in other Chinese cities. It was said that visitors felt exposed—perhaps agoraphobic—when they were in Shanghai.

Yu Yuan Gardens, view c. 1920
The English colonials generally resisted the charms of anything Chinese, but the gardens of Shanghai were an exception. The expats were, as one writer expressed, "delighted with the curious bridges" and they marveled at the timeless splendors of the Ten-Thousand-Flower Pavilion and Hall of Jade Magnificence.

Longhua Pagoda
The pagoda form, with its turned-up eaves, represents the belief that the earth is rectilinear but the heavens are round. Longhua, one of Shanghai's most striking examples of traditional architecture, is among its few remaining pagodas. Dating to the third century but renovated many times since, its current style reflects the structure as it was in 977, during the Song dynasty. During World War II, Japanese forces used the pagoda as an antiaircraft gun emplacement, one of Shanghai's lingering grievances.

The Bund, c. 1900
The Shanghainese call the riverfront district Waitan, but Westerners still refer to it as the Bund (which means "embankment" in Hindi), a name that harks back to the period when English gunboats and trading vessels dominated Shanghai's waterfront. The era of European colonialism is as indelibly imprinted in the Bund's architecture as in its name.

Shanghai's powerful merchants' guilds developed commercial centers with pagodalike lodges called *huiguans*, used for official business, administration, education, and worship. Few *huiguans* remain in Shanghai, though a rare example can be seen in the Hu Xin Ting Pavilion, now a teahouse, in the restored Yu Yuan Gardens. The "willow-patterned teahouse," as the English called it, was built in 1784 for dealers of blue-dyed cotton. It is typical of classic Chinese pavilion architecture: The structure is spare; brackets are prominent, intricately carved, and colorful; and the roof has upturned eaves, a common lyrical device reflecting the Chinese cosmic view of the earth as rectilinear, the heavens as circular. The eaves outline the curves that delineate the heavens and accentuate the weightlessness of the unearthly world above. The building is still connected to a zigzag bridge, a characteristic form for ceremonial structures and a symbolic deterrent to evil spirits that are said to travel only in straight lines.

SHANGHAI HAS ALWAYS attracted outsiders. Among those who stayed, those of longest standing and greatest significance were the British, whose propensity for navigation and trade brought them to the port city in the 1830s. The Qing dynasty rulers were isolationists but—weakened by internal divisions, insurrections, famines, and economic stagnation—were ultimately unable to stem the encroachment of foreign power. The British were enthusiastic colonialists but they initially struggled with a trade deficit: The Chinese did not want or need British textiles and other goods as much as Britons demanded Chinese tea and spices. The discovery and manufacture of opium, extracted from poppy fields in British colonies in India, quickly reversed the imbalance, at China's woeful expense. Chinese attempts to curtail the drug trade led to the Opium Wars, the rout of Chinese ports by the English fleet, and the 1842 Treaty of Nanjing, which ceded Hong Kong to Britain and put trade zones under British jurisdiction in other ports, the most important of which was Shanghai.

Hu Xin Ting Pavilion

Hu Xin Ting was a guildhall, built in 1784. It was known in English as the "willow-patterned teahouse" for its resemblance to a pottery pattern popular in England. Today it is the centerpiece of Yu Yuan Gardens, a Ming-period enclave that is now a public park. The zigzag bridge leading to Hu Xin Ting was designed to confound evil spirits. It's an early example of the role of symbolism in Chinese architecture.

English-style villa, International Settlement, 1930s

Villa Ghisi, French Concession, c. 1920s

Bungalow, French Concession, 1917

During Shanghai's prolonged prewar economic boom, the architectural fantasies of well-off European and Chinese residents revolved around the English estate style. Many houses were designed with Chinese touches, such as carved eaves and brackets. Shanghai's diverse residential architecture also included simple Craftsman-style bungalows—low-pitched houses that proliferated in America in the early twentieth century—which found their way to China via design magazines and Western architects mining for commissions.

The trade zones guaranteed foreigners the right to own property, make their own laws, and largely ignore Chinese authority. A semicolonial situation quickly took root in Shanghai, as the British and the French laid claim to sectors of the city. The British took a preeminent waterfront site, creating the English Settlement along the Huangpu River and Suzhou Creek in 1843. (Twenty years later the English Settlement would merge with the adjacent American Zone, forming the International Settlement.) It was a choice location for commerce, and English banks and trading companies soon lined the west bank of the Huangpu. The smaller French Concession, created just south of the English Settlement in 1849, had a different cast, with leafy residential boulevards. On the edge of those two districts, tucked within remnants of the ancient city wall, the old Chinese city remained a tight web of streets, houses, markets, and gardens. It was filled with "curious bridges, gateways, gigantic lamps, grottoes, shady alcoves, and . . . rockery," in the words of a British visitor in 1852.

Yet none of Shanghai's districts was more architecturally prominent than the International Settlement, largely because of the British influence but also because of its setting along the broad sweep of waterfront called the Bund. The name, derived from a Hindi word for "embankment," has survived as a mark of the colonial era. The earliest British buildings on the Bund were in a simple hybrid style called "compradoric." (The term is a reference to the compradors, Chinese who had mastered pidgin—a corruption of the word "business"—English and served as liaisons between Europeans and native workers.) Usually of wood-frame or brick construction, the buildings featured broad verandas, pitched roofs, and sometimes a widow's walk. Although contemporary European accounts described them as having a "grand and imposing appearance," the airy, almost tropical-looking structures were neither grand nor indigenous in design. They probably derived from a similar type devised for India or South China, as they were undeniably ill-suited to Shanghai's cold, damp winters. By the end of the nineteenth century most had been replaced by monumental beaux arts structures that made the Bund resemble a capital of the British Empire more than a neighborhood in China.

ARMED WITH THEIR special privileges and backed by military might, the Europeans expanded their zones in Shanghai. The International Settlement pushed west into the countryside, by request of the Chinese imperial court and by authority of the British gunboats permanently docked in Shanghai Harbor. In 1898 France extended its concession by having a company of soldiers demolish the walls of a cemetery to make way for a new road. The soldiers then quelled a riot of angry Chinese with force that killed at least twelve people.

As Europeans' ambitions for growth blurred the boundaries of the once-distinct zones, so too did the surging Chinese population. Rebellions elsewhere in the country led many Chinese to seek refuge in the settlements, where Western police and troops generally kept chaos at bay. By 1910 some 617,000 Chinese lived in the settlements, constituting almost two-thirds of the population there; another 675,000 Chinese inhabited the rest of Shanghai. Finally, in 1912, the walls around the old Chinese city came down too, signaling an end to attempts to keep the three zones physically and ethnically separate. Europeans and Chinese already lived on the same streets and shopped in the same stores, although they rarely interacted on anything but the most rudimentary level.

Still, there was a history of undeniable tension between the Shanghainese (natives) and Shanghailanders (Western residents). The Sikh policemen who pa-trolled the International Settlement on behalf of the British were famously cruel, beating rickshaw coolies to a bitter pulp for minor traffic infractions. For the "red-haired devils," as Europeans were sometimes called, ignorance of Chinese ways became a source of pride. Taking an interest in Chinese culture was considered an eccentricity, and anything more than basic dealings with natives was regarded as déclassé. In the early years, social mixing was so strongly frowned on that a special fund was maintained for the purpose of shipping home destitute Europeans, who were considered at risk of "going Chinese." Yet towering hypocrisy characterized European attitudes. Many bigoted "China hands" kept native mistresses and often fathered children by them.

The decadence of expatriate life in Shanghai grew in direct proportion to the city's affluence. By the end of the nineteenth century, Shanghai had acquired a reputation as the world's most licentious city, filled with brothels, gambling houses, and opium dens. Nevertheless, a predictable decorousness remained entrenched. There were the continuous games of cricket, lawn bowling, racquets, and other sports. In 1872 the British consul wrote of the typical Englishman in Shanghai as having great wealth but an empty existence: "He builds himself a mansion in the handsomest style that his firm or himself can afford, and he furnishes it as a rule with homemade [British] furniture, plate, glass, etc., all the best quality. . . . He drives a pretentious vehicle with a pair of Cape, Australian or California horses. . . . After the evening airing comes dinner, and it is in this meal that the foreign resident in China concentrates his efforts to forget that he is an exile from home." One English businessman in this period bluntly expressed his disdain for his temporary residence when he wrote, "In two or three years at farthest, I hope to realize a fortune and to get away. You must not expect men of my situation to condemn themselves to years of prolonged exile in an unhealthy climate for the benefit of posterity."

Life changed for Europeans in the decades that followed, but insular attitudes did not abate. As late as the 1930s, foreign correspondents in Shanghai were shocked by the ignorance of the Europeans who sat in their clubs, drank gin, and carried on about the "real" situation in China, which was then on the brink of disaster. John Gunther put it this way in *Inside Asia* (1939): "In Shanghai one finds most flamboyantly and conspicuously the Westerner who hates the Chinese." The reason? "He has done the Chinese an injury, that is sucked the wealth out of him, for this he cannot forgive China."

While the domineering presence of foreigners was an irritation, and worse, for local society, the Europeans and Chinese did share some values. Both prized the Bund; its beauty was and continues to be a source of pride. Its buildings are unmistakably European, but its splendor harks back to a rule enacted in the middle 1800s by the *taotai*, or local imperial administrator. He decreed that a towpath be maintained along the river to a width of at least thirty feet. That provided sufficient passage for wagons at the time, which was probably what the *taotai* had in mind, but his edict had lasting architectural benefits. One British resident gave the early Chinese magistrate his due for keeping "all-devouring commerce" at bay. "Had commerce had its way, we should not have been able to boast that our Bund is one of the handsomest streets in the world," wrote the Reverend Charles Ewart Darwent in 1920.

For their part, the Chinese appreciated some European landmarks for particular and unexpected reasons. The first British-built Custom House, which went up in 1893, may not have impressed with its genteel Gothic Revival design, but the

Chinese were amused by the bell in the 110-foot clock tower. Clock towers were something new in China—they enforced a strictly European concept of time. This one's ringing, every fifteen minutes, was initially inexplicable, but Shanghainese came to appreciate it as a protection against fire. Fire was the usual reason for any public tolling of bells, and the Chinese liked to think that all the ringing was fooling the fire gods to believe that Shanghai was burning quite enough.

BY THE EARLY TWENTIETH century, Shanghai's bustling trade was making not just the Europeans rich, but many Chinese as well. They too took to building Tudor-style houses on parklike estates on the outskirts of the International Settlement. The travel writer Edward Park marveled in this period at the extravagant life-styles of monied Chinese. He wrote that they traveled with "their whole harems, grandmothers, daughters, nurses, womankind generally, decked out in the most gorgeous of silks and satins, glossy black hair, well-greased and heavily laden with gold tines, flowers, jade, and kingfishers' feathers. . . . Everyone seems so happy that one forgets the dust, the noise, and even the danger."

Among the most famous and successful Chinese businessmen was Charlie Soong, whose life encapsulated the profound change shaping his country from the last decades of the feudal Qing dynasty (1644–1912) through the rise of

Embankment House
PALMER AND TURNER, 1933
Small rivers such as Suzhou Creek were essential to shipping and local commerce. In the 1930s the Suzhou's banks were built up with warehouses, factories, and modern apartment buildings such as the Embankment House, one example of Shanghai's surviving collection of Art Deco architecture.

Nationalism. The son of small merchants from the interior, he became patriarch of one of China's most influential families. His parents were ambitious enough to send him to America, about 1880. He first worked in a Boston tea shop, then studied theology in a Methodist seminary in North Carolina. He was a sharp student and regretted leaving America at the end of his studies, when he was sent to Shanghai as a Christian missionary. The evangelical life turned out to be only partly satisfying for the energetic Soong, but he used it as an entrée to business, manufacturing and selling Bibles. He succeeded over the next few years as a printer, a flour mill manager, and an agent for imported machinery.

Soong earned a fair fortune but chose to live in unspectacular circumstances in a French Concession town house described as part Western, part Chinese. His son and three daughters, all educated in America, would greatly expand the family's prestige and power. (At one time his son, a financier and politician, was thought to be the world's wealthiest man.) About 1910 Soong met Sun Yat-sen, the Nationalist revolutionary who would be elected provisional president of the new Republic of China in 1911. Sun, enchanted by Soong's daughters, hired one as his secretary and married another. In some ways this marriage symbolized the contradictory alliance of the Nationalists, who preached rejection of Western values, and their financial backers among the rich bourgeoisie of Shanghai.

Soong's youngest daughter, Mei-ling, became a striking embodiment of that contradiction. As a girl Mei-ling frequently complained to her father that their house was too small. He refused to buy a mansion, but Mei-ling bought one herself after her father died. Single and conspicuously self-reliant, Mei-ling was a social phenomenon in cosmopolitan Shanghai, with her degree in English literature and casual attire of tennis togs, which she wore around the house. In 1927 she married Chiang Kai-shek, who became president of the Nationalist government the following year. As first lady, Madame Chiang wielded considerable political power, but the role also enabled her to indulge her taste for high heels, fur coats, and, as the writer John Gunther put it, an "expensive state of mind." For Madame Chiang and many Chinese, the modernity they aspired to was decidedly Western in character.

SHANGHAI IN THE 1920s and 1930s was home to a politically volatile mix of Europeans, Nationalists, Communists, warlords, and gangsters, but the city glittered with the trappings of a hugely prosperous golden age: Motorcars roared past modern banks, big houses, and glitzy nightclubs. The year 1929 came and went, and the Great Depression hardly touched the city. Its manorial life-style continued, its underworld and its opium dens were as active as ever, and an expatriate

City Lights Apartments
BREGMAN + HAMANN, 2003
Toronto-based Bregman + Hamann is one of the many Western firms involved in Shanghai's contemporary building boom. B+H designed City Lights, an apartment complex in the downtown Jinan district, with an eye to the streamlined Art Deco style for which Shanghai provides abundant inspiration.

community still diverted itself with horse racing, costume balls, and prostitution of dazzling variety. It was as if Shanghai's surpassing self-indulgence protected the place from the larger threats of economic collapse and simmering world war. But when disaster hit, it hit with unusual force.

Shanghai at the onset of World War II is chronicled in heartrending fashion in J. G. Ballard's 1984 novel *Empire of the Sun*. Ballard's autobiographical story, about a child separated from his parents on December 8, 1941, is told from the point of view of eleven-year-old Jim. As the boy wanders deserted homes in search of safety, Ballard depicts Shanghai as a latter-day Pompeii. Jim ambles into lavish villas with abandoned pools and overgrown lawns. He finds a place to sleep for a night or two in sleek apartments in the French Concession. The frightening picaresque continues until the occupying Japanese troops, who have arrested all the adults, finally pick up Jim too.

Shanghai fell into decay and worse in the decades that followed the war, and, as in Ballard's tale, the architecture provided an important backdrop to years of hard Communist rule. The student cadres of the Cultural Revolution coursed through the streets to break down wrought-iron gates and invade the splendid homes where, they were certain, only "running dogs" of capitalism lived.

It was China's bad fortune that the wealthy Shanghainese who lived in Tudor Revival houses and the like often filled them with priceless Chinese treasures—furniture and art, scrolls, ancient porcelains—which the intruding students destroyed. Many works of Chinese art were lost forever, but much of the European-inspired architecture survived. Houses were aggressively carved up into workers' apartments. During the bleak years of repression, these houses and gardens were reminders of a gentler past, feeding a nostalgia few dared to express.

IN 1979, when Deng Xiaoping, China's leader after Mao's death three years earlier, announced the Open Door policy, a new blueprint for foreign trade and economic development in China began to evolve. Plans to bring China onto center stage economically were complex, political, abstract, and quixotic. But everyone agreed that economic development would be accompanied by a building campaign.

Shanghai was left out of the early schemes for economic growth, which highlighted free-trade zones and tax abatements for cities in the south, most of them close to Hong Kong. Shanghai was still China's traditional center of industry, but to admire it openly in communist circles was to suggest questionable support for capitalistic decadence. At the outset of the Open Door years Shanghai was considered "old, worn out, and sluggish," according to one academic report on the subject. More aggressive plans to develop Shanghai did not arrive until the early 1990s.

Despite Beijing's neglect, Shanghai's leaders had their own ambitions for the city. They revived an old Nationalist idea to develop a new district, Pudong—literally, "east of the river"—as Shanghai's modern commercial center but recognized that it required planning on a scale unprecedented in China. Shanghai's mayor made a tour of European cities and was most impressed by La Défense, the modern business district on the edge of Paris. His visit inspired an important relationship between French and Chinese planners.

But developing comprehensive urban schemes takes time, so Shanghai's officials proposed a gesture inspired less by the city's impulse to plan the future than by its impatience to get there: a new television tower, not complicated in engineering terms but of a height and form to prove that their intentions were serious. The tower would serve not only for television transmission (in fact, it soon became obsolete for that purpose) but as a centerpiece for Pudong. In 1986 municipal bureaucrats and television technocrats took the wholly unfamiliar step of staging a competition for the tower's design. Some of China's largest architectural institutes (studios closely linked to the state) were invited to participate, and the commission went to Shanghai Modern Architectural Design Company. The tower was to rise fifteen hundred feet—at more than four times the height of any structure then in China, a real challenge for Chinese architects. Lin Den-li, the lead designer on the project, explained that the team looked at other television towers around the world—in Moscow, Tokyo, and Toronto, among other cities—but that no real models for the project existed. "We were to treat this commission not just as a building but as a work of art," he said, "and a work of art must be original."

Three preliminary proposals were for a building Lin described as a "long-stemmed flower," a single-column tower, and another tower suggesting a series of globes ascending in the sky. After a long selection process, the jury chose the spherical scheme, resulting in the Oriental Pearl Television Tower. The reasons for the verdict were never known; then as now, China's design competitions were politically charged and opaque.

Although the architects had considered the flowerlike scheme the most beautiful, Lin defended the winning design, saying it was inspired by the Eiffel Tower, with a base that spreads out and defines an outdoor space. At the same time, he admitted that the tower might have taken another form had it been accompanied by urban planning. As Pudong evolved, the main parkland was sited elsewhere. "And if we had known how many tall buildings were going to go up around it," Lin said, "we might have chosen a different shape." As it is, the Oriental Pearl Television Tower, completed in 1995, has a primitive look despite futuristic intent and is most frequently described as "kitsch." The world's third-tallest structure, it struggles to break free of an architectural tradition entrenched in the Brutalism of reinforced concrete.

Shanghai's true entry to the modern age did not come until Beijing lent its support in 1992. The turning point was Deng Xiaoping's southern tour of China, which included a series of speeches calling for economic reform. He was semi-retired, and his successors did not completely agree with him about encouraging free enterprise or allowing foreign investment. But Deng was insistent, and the Shanghai stop on his tour was key. He declared that Shanghai would lead China's modernization, that the city would be the head of the great dragon of new wealth that could stretch from the mouth of the Yangtze River throughout the interior. "Change every year," declared Deng, "and big changes every three years."

Oriental Pearl Television Tower
SHANGHAI MODERN ARCHITECTURAL
DESIGN COMPANY, 1995
The Oriental Pearl Television Tower, the world's third-tallest structure, was Shanghai's first attempt to create an instantly recognizable architectural signature. It was intended to be the centerpiece of a large park, which was later built in another part of Pudong. The tower's base defines an open space in the financial district.

Pudong streets
Pudong's newest buildings vie for attention not only with distinctive architectural detail but also with flashy signage.

Beijing held back at first, suppressing many of Deng's speeches on the theme. But later that year Shanghai was added to a list of special economic zones that could offer economic incentives to attract foreign capital. In 1992 and 1993 Shanghai's municipal administration invited urbanists from Europe and Japan to study Pudong and propose concepts for its orderly development. The initial project comprised the few acres directly across from the Bund: A mile-square area by the river, it would encompass forty million square feet of office space and make up Pudong's central commercial section, Lujiazui. Four distinguished architect-planners—Massimiliano Fuksas, Richard Rogers, Toyo Ito, and Dominique Perrault—made a series of trips to Shanghai to imagine the future, but their work had little influence on the maps eventually produced by the Shanghai Planning Institute. Strangely, foundations were being dug for major skyscrapers even before the plans were settled. "Why a skyscraper there?" Fuksas asked. "That's where the investors want it," replied municipal officials.

Those early investors were often from Hong Kong, Taiwan, and the Chinese community in the United States. For them, the promise of free enterprise in China—a market of 1.5 billion potential consumers—had been a long time in coming. Their eagerness coupled with that of the long-repressed entrepreneurs on the mainland. With the combination of pent-up economic energy and top-down economic planning—the capitalist and communist engines of China's new growth—Pudong exploded. It was said that half the world's construction cranes were at work in Shanghai by the turn of the millennium. As foreign investment poured in, American and European architects were invited to compete for commissions. Since Chinese law demanded that most architectural commissions be awarded after a design competition, the number of Western architects who were exposed to China and tempted to work there grew geometrically.

One was Jean-Marie Charpentier, a Parisian who arrived in Shanghai in the early 1990s and whose experiences encapsulated the difficulties of practicing architecture there. Charpentier had worked in Cambodia as a professor at the School of Architecture in Phnom Penh, then aided the government's effort to have the archaeological zone of Angkor Wat declared a UNESCO World Heritage site; eventually he landed a commission for a large tourist hotel nearby. The Cambodian projects reinforced his view that "architecture has a dual dimension. It is local, culture-based, and vernacular, but it is also international, universal, and flexible."

Yet ten years of work elsewhere in Asia failed to prepare Charpentier for the challenges he would encounter in Shanghai. In the mid-1990s, for instance, he was awarded first place in a competition for an international exposition center in Pudong. Then he learned he would receive the commission only if he could involve French investors. As he could not, the commission went to the architect Helmut Jahn, who brought a German convention management group into the project.

**Shanghai Urban Planning
Exhibition Centre**
SHANGHAI MODERN ARCHITECTURAL
DESIGN COMPANY, 1998
The Chinese designers of this
museum and exhibit hall, set on
a prominent site on a corner of
People's Park, set out to match the
scale and vigor of the Grand Theater
at the other end of the park.
The architecture was inspired by a
flower form.

Aurora Plaza
The facade of the Aurora Plaza building, completed in 2003, gleams with reflective gold in the daytime but becomes a sixteen-story video screen at night.

Nanpu Bridge
BUCKLAND & TAYLOR WITH SHANGHAI MUNICIPAL ENGINEERING DESIGN INSTITUTE, 1991
Only tunnels and a ferry connected Shanghai's west and east banks (Puxi and Pudong) before the 1990s, when bridges were built to span the Huangpu River. The Nanpu Bridge, which extends more than five miles, has a spiraling access ramp on the Puxi side. Drivers deplore it, but the compact corkscrew design was a way to conserve precious land.

Charpentier next entered a competition for the Grand Theater, a major project inspired, it was said, by the late premier Chou En-lai's love of European opera. The building's immense importance was implicit in its site; it would dominate a corner of People's Park, a new public green space where the European racetrack had been. Next door was a new municipal administration building, an early, bland attempt by Chinese architects at sleek modernism. Also nearby was the old Jockey Club, a splendid Victorian building that since World War II had served as a morgue, a warehouse, and lately as the Shanghai Art Museum.

The project demanded a high-profile design that would compensate for the drab municipal building and overshadow the Jockey Club's overt Anglocentrism. Charpentier's scheme included a bowl atop the roof, a feature inspired by rooftop gardens at Versailles in France. But as he presented his competition drawings—which he did with lyrical descriptions written by a Chinese poet—the architect explained how the design evoked the metaphor of the circular heavens over the rectilinear earth. With his blend of Western architecture and Chinese imagery, Charpentier was declared the winner among eighteen entrants, and this time municipal administrators prepared a contract for him within twenty-four hours.

But the deal came with many encumbrances: Onerous deadlines, penalties, and other difficulties made the architect wonder if he had won a design competition or was about to lose his practice. Construction began before any but the most rudimentary details had been determined. Engineering and shop drawings, usually made in sequence, were prepared more or less simultaneously, and the whole project became an exercise in improvisation. Charpentier had intended lightweight framing, but hull builders from the shipyards were called in for the

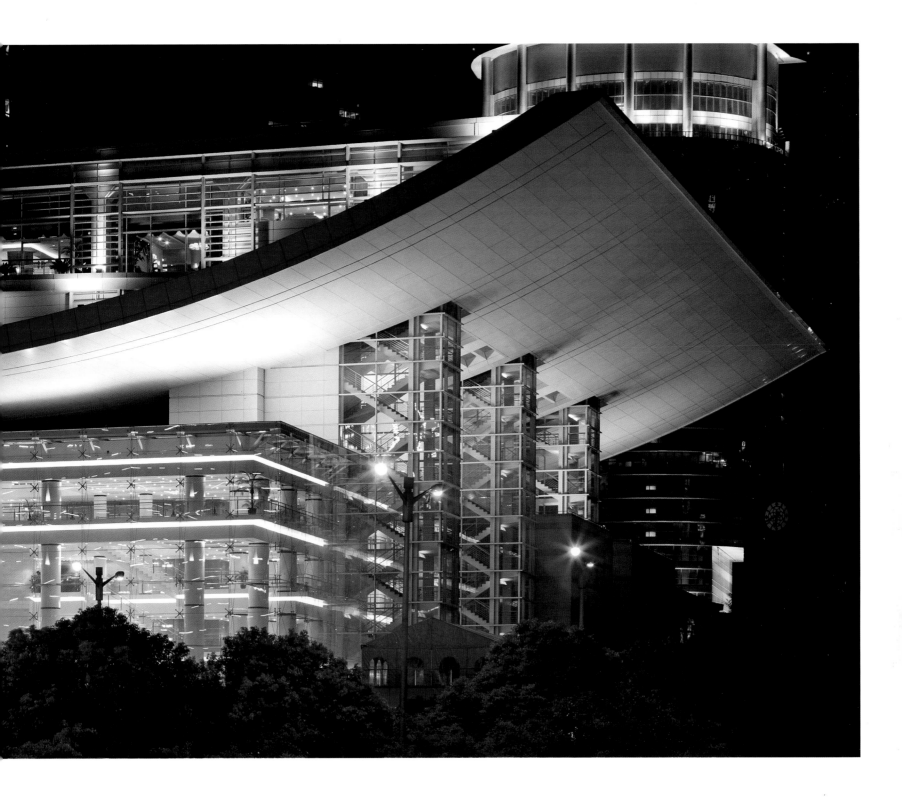

job. Great steel trusses, twice as heavy as the entire Eiffel Tower, were assembled on the ground and hoisted into place over six concrete cores.

Nevertheless, the Grand Theater dazzled China when it opened in 1998. It also demonstrated the ability of Charpentier's studio to succeed under haphazard conditions, a skill that led to other significant projects. The next was a plan for Century Avenue, a three-mile boulevard running through Pudong from the river to a park and government center. Charpentier's thoroughfare, wide as a football field, brought some order to Pudong, which had until then developed ad hoc. Instead of the expressway Shanghai planners had envisioned, Charpentier included intersections and gardens, intended to be inviting to pedestrians. Only time will tell if Century Avenue becomes the Champs-Élysées of Shanghai, as Charpentier intended and officials already boast.

Shanghai Grand Theater
ARTE CHARPENTIER, 1998
With its glassy exterior and upturned roof, the Grand Theater suggests great lightness, though it was constructed of massive iron trusses. Its transparency, achieved with a cable-net glass curtain wall, makes views of the city part of the spectacle and allows the theater's glow to animate Shanghai at night.

Shanghai Grand Theater
The coolly modern Grand Theater, raised on a pedestal, is one of the new architectural icons that define People's Park.

Auditorium, Shanghai Grand Theater
The building houses three theaters, the largest of which seats eighteen hundred. The first performance, by the National Ballet of China, was *Swan Lake*.

Lobby, Shanghai Grand Theater
The Grand Theater's interiors, including its soaring lobby (opposite), reflect Shanghai's newfound fascination with daring engineering and vertiginous height.

People's Park

The horse racing track where English and American residents once diverted themselves with the sport of kings was converted into People's Park (below) in 1952. It was further transformed by a spate of recent construction. One of the first new buildings was the blandly modern city hall (at far right), which went up in the early 1990s. It was followed by the more exuberant architecture of the Grand Theater (center) in 1998 and Tomorrow Square (the tallest tower shown) in 2003.

"Big hat" buildings

A number of the buildings that rose about the turn of the twentieth century were undistinguished except for their extraordinary upper stories—an extension of the Chinese tendency to top conventional structures with "big hats," or pagodalike roofs. Among the most eye-catching is the Bund Center's crown (John Portman & Associates, 2002, opposite, near right). Other buildings are capped by postmodern exuberance such as the grain silo atop China Merchants Tower (Simon Kwan & Associates, 1995, center), and the Art Deco melange reflected in a glass curtain wall near the Bund (far right).

With thousands of new buildings rising up around Century Avenue and all across the city, Shanghai had in less than a decade acquired the "largest concentration of skyscrapers in the world," according to the English-language *China Daily* in 2001. But the building boom slowed—by government decree—in 2003. Among the reasons cited were the needs to temporarily brake an overheated economy, guard against a dangerous real estate "bubble," and control the slight but perceptible sinking of the earth beneath Shanghai under the weight of so much new construction.

Simultaneous with the reassessment of the appropriate amount of construction was a reevaluation of the appropriate type: A backlash began to emerge against the gaudy architecture that had filled the city so quickly. Developers who had once insisted on buildings that drew attention to themselves started to appreciate design's relationship to long-term function and economics. At the same time, architects were accusing one another of designing costly and visually disruptive "white elephants" and of purveying "secondhand architecture"—wild schemes that had been rejected in the West. Such debate reflected a budding awareness of architecture's impact on the cityscape, which led in turn to a newly mature approach and more restrained results. By 2005 the new skyscrapers going up were less aggressively unusual and entirely more interesting.

WITH STAGGERING SPEED, change has touched every corner of Shanghai, from the famed Bund to futuristic Pudong, and from Puxi, the city's core, to the distant outskirts, where brand-new suburbs are rising. The course of development in each area variously reflects the still unresolved tensions between capitalism and communism, East and West, large-scale construction and preservation. Thus Shanghai's architecture provides an acute lens through which to examine this ancient trading port's complex history, its evolution from prosperous colonial outpost to drab industrial center, and its dazzling metamorphosis into one of the most ambitious, vibrant, and significant "new" cities of the twenty-first century.

PAST AND PRESENT ON THE BUND

THE 1920S ROARED in Shanghai as in few other cities in the world. A glamorous, extravagant golden age had taken hold about World War I, when the port city filled the commercial vacuum left by disruptions in Europe. Ensconced in palatial headquarters, local banks and other businesses generated unprecedented wealth. Well-dressed people thronged the sidewalks and the streetcars. The city had embraced a twentieth-century modernity of motorcars, movie houses, and social mobility.

Despite the good times, there were ominous signs of an underlying instability. A civil war raged a few hundred miles away; Japanese troops were encroaching on outlying territory, laying the groundwork for attack; and workers were organizing strident protests. But up until its collapse with the onset of World War II, Shanghai flourished. It was compared to Paris for its luster and to Manhattan for its skyward growth.

Art Deco apartments and streamlined skyscrapers would remake the skyline elsewhere in Shanghai during the Jazz Age, but tradition reigned along the stately Bund, with its architectural evocations of Britannia's colonial past. Even today, most of the Bund reflects the neoclassical style of the Shanghai Club, at the south end, where the British taipans, or corporate chiefs, finished their not-overlong workday with drinks and badinage. The clubhouse, as pretentious and squat as many of its members, was designed by English architect B. H. Tarrand and completed in 1910. Outside were granite columns and a pair of towers; inside was the "longest bar in the world," 110 feet. Within this bastion of privilege, each member's social status was defined by how close to the front of the club room he was permitted to sit.

Comfortably retrograde, Shanghai's English business class resisted change. Ambitious architects may have been eager to move past overelaborate, obsolete neoclassical styles like the so-called Shanghai Renaissance but were thwarted by their clients' fossilized conservatism. The firm that finally managed to bring twentieth-century architecture to the Bund did so by concealing innovative construction in buildings that appeared to be classical. With that approach, and with particular skill, Palmer and Turner came to own the Bund architecturally by the end of the golden age. Its most grandiose building on the Bund was the Hongkong and Shanghai Bank (HSBC), completed in 1923.

The Bund
Once an imposing Anglocentric business district, the Bund has become a popular promenade, proudly reclaimed by the Shanghainese

The Bund, 1930s
The Bund expressed the British colonial ethos well into the twentieth century, with Europeans living and working in grand buildings at some remove from the Chinese toiling outside. Yet the splendid avenue along the Bund (above) was preserved by the decree of a mid-1880s Chinese governor, without whose foresight the riverfront might easily have been sold off and developed.

The Bund, 1880
This view (left) shows the Huangpu, typically active with ships, and the riverbank lined with compradoric architecture. The style was named for the native Chinese managers and contractors who knew just enough English to get along in business. Although the buildings were typical of Great Britain's Asian colonies of the period, their wood frames and verandas were ill suited to cold Shanghai winters, and they were soon replaced.

Shanghai Club

B. H. TARRAND, 1910

The original Shanghai Club (top), built in 1864, was a compradoric mansion larger and more pretentious than others on the Bund. Within a half century, the treaty port's great wealth and the English residents' longing for home had inspired an even grander successor (right), along with the Bund's other beaux arts palaces.

Palmer and Turner had a decadeslong history with HSBC. Back in the 1880s, the architects who would later form the firm were lured from England to design the bank's headquarters in Hong Kong. That grand, enormous building was rightly compared to London's Bank of England for the splendor of its Queen's Road facade. But the architects deftly added a local touch, a side wing in the compradoric style—more open, less imposing, and suited to both natives and foreigners working or doing business there. The design was seen as a successful blend for bicultural Hong Kong, and as a result Palmer and Turner served as HSBC's architect for the next half century.

The bank's new building in Shanghai was by George Leopold Wilson, Palmer and Turner's chief designer there. An architect with a modern turn of mind, Wilson wrote that he deplored "unessentials in the nature of flamboyant ornaments, heavy cornices and applied features, such as classic orders." A graduate of the Surveyors Institute in England, he had moved to Hong Kong to work for Palmer and Turner; at the onset of World War I, when turmoil in Europe turned out to be a boon for business in China, the firm sent him to Shanghai. Wilson went out on his own shortly after arriving but often worked with Palmer and Turner. The buildings he designed, mostly on the Bund, became icons of both the firm and the city.

Wilson's first major project in Shanghai, the Union Assurance Building (1914), was richly ornamented to satisfy the clients, but beneath the surface was the city's first steel-frame office building. This modern technology allowed for a larger structure and a more flexible, light-filled interior than would have been possible with a load-bearing masonry wall, especially in Shanghai, whose location on the Yangtze River Delta made for a wet, unstable base.

The Hongkong and Shanghai Bank, begun several years later, was intended as a commanding manifestation of the client's preeminence in Asian banking. Grandeur was the goal, and as the design took shape on the drawing boards at Palmer and Turner's Shanghai office, the architects did not hesitate to request a larger construction budget. The client's response was unambiguous: "Spare no expense, but dominate the Bund." The bank's taste was for a long, imposing palazzo. Its aspect was antique, yet it was conceived with many features seen in modern commercial buildings in the United States. Among the innovations used was a concrete slab foundation, developed some years before in Chicago, another boomtown with a soggy bottom.

"The soil is practically liquid mud," wrote Wilson of his Shanghai site. He hoped that the concrete slab foundation, called a "floating raft," would help distribute the building's weight over the marshy land, so that the building would settle gradually and evenly over time. Wilson's engineering calculations proved accurate, and a good thing it was. When constructed, the first granite step of

Union Assurance Building
Palmer and Turner, 1914
The building's beaux arts profile and its richly carved granite ornament conveyed the grandeur essential to its occupant, an English financial concern. Yet the large windows, strong vertical lines, and relative lightness reveal a modern sensibility and up-to-date construction beneath the surface.

the building's entrance was placed six feet above grade; not long after completion, it had settled to be level with the sidewalk. Other up-to-date construction techniques, including the use of reinforced concrete, were employed and many modern features, such as elevators, plumbing cores, and light wells, were incorporated. Ventilation and air conditioning provided a pleasant surprise during Shanghai's steamy summers: Fresh air ran through cool water so that room temperatures never exceeded eighty degrees Fahrenheit.

The stately facade also was influenced by modernity, albeit subtly. The bank was hardly streamlined but it did have a simplified profile influenced by John Soane, architect for London's Bank of England, who took neoclassicism to the edge of modernity. It also had flattened surfaces inspired by American commercial architecture. There were other interesting touches, such as the dome, which was pushed toward the front, foreshortening its perspective and intensifying its effect from the street below. This device was not strictly modern; it was used in the 1600s in Borromini's Church of Sant'Agnese in Rome. But it did suggest Wilson's flexible sense of proportion, not ubiquitous in classic European architecture at the time and downright rare in Shanghai.

Nonetheless, the building's modernity was largely undetected by passersby. Inside were the predictable marble-laden banking rooms, with columns, mosaic floors, and colorful frescoes with classical subjects. All that pomp was entirely in keeping with HSBC's reputation as Asia's leading financial institution in this period of extravagant wealth. But along with those evocations of ancient Rome were reflections of the East. In the Chinese departments, where local people were likely to conduct business, "one is arrested on the threshold by the totally unexpected sight of a blaze of Chinese decoration," according to a booklet published to accompany the building's opening. "While the design, both in the mass and the details, is entirely new, one feels the influence of the best traditions of fourteenth century Chinese art in this gorgeous Oriental decoration of a hall of twentieth century Western construction." Wilson's predilection for the modern, like Frank Lloyd Wright's, turned out to be in harmony with the spareness of traditional Asian interiors.

The sobriety of the HSBC building belied the tenor of Shanghai in the Jazz Age, when it was one of the world's most lubricious cities. But contradictions were everywhere in Shanghai. It was simultaneously known as the "Paris of the East" and the "whore of the Orient." The bronze lions flanking the bank entrance were reputed to roar whenever a virgin passed on the sidewalk; their silence suggested only that the lions were waiting patiently for one to walk by.

The slow transition from the Shanghai Renaissance style to modern skyscrapers took another step with the new Custom House, built on the site of the previous one, next door to the HSBC bank. Palmer and Taylor designed it for the Municipal Council, which governed the International Settlement and oversaw the collection of duties on behalf of the Chinese. Asserting lavish architectural dominance of the Bund was less important for this building than it had been for the bank; the architect, Edwin Forbes Bothwell, appeared more concerned with emulating—in profile, if not in height—the skyscrapers going up in America. Its ten stories plus a clock tower made the Custom House the city's tallest building when it was completed in 1928. The clock tower, which added the equivalent of five to six stories to the height, complicated the engineering of the concrete slab foundation. It required 225 extra fifty-foot piles directly beneath it, plus precise calculations to assure that its tons of steel and granite would settle at the same

Hongkong and Shanghai Banking Corporation Headquarters
PALMER AND TURNER, 1923
Despite its backward-looking form—a plutocrat's palace—the Hongkong and Shanghai Bank had many modern characteristics, including a raft-type foundation to distribute the building's great weight over the swampy soil; large and open interior spaces; and up-to-date heating, ventilation, and air conditioning systems.

The bank's central hall is octagonal, addressing the Chinese belief in the number eight's promise of good fortune; it also is laden with European decor. The classical rotunda's dome, fifty-three feet in diameter, is supported by Siena marble. Venetian mosaic decorates the floor and the dome. A 1997 renovation uncovered the panels around the entablature. They symbolically depict eight great banking centers: London is represented by the

mythological figure "Britannia," Paris by the "Republic," and Shanghai by "Sagacity."

During the Cultural Revolution (1966–76) the bank served as Shanghai's city hall. It now houses the Shanghai Pudong Development Bank, along with the offices of many private companies. The 1997 renovation restored the banking rooms' antique splendor and modern flow.

rate as the rest of the building. The English-language *Far Eastern Review* reported that the new Custom House was "massive in design, massive in structural detail, and massive in size," all considered positive characteristics in China.

Bothwell's design saw to it that sheer size was accompanied by the sleek lines that were de rigueur in American commercial architecture. Flat surfaces, verticality, simplified classical ornament, and towering height marked it as modern. A large central light court also made the Custom House similar to American skyscrapers in terms of floor plan and abundant natural light. There were administrative rooms on lower floors, offices above, and apartments for officials and their servants from the sixth through tenth story. Sophisticated architectural touches were overshadowed by the clock tower called "Big Ching," the largest timepiece in Shanghai.

George Wilson occasionally wrote about the Shanghai design scene in the monthly *China Journal of Science and the Arts* and in 1934 marveled at Shanghai's transformation, some of which was his doing. "The skyline in every direction has completely changed," he wrote. "Shanghai is a new city as compared with the Shanghai of a few years ago." He was impressed by the infrastructure improvements, including roads and public utilities; he was also attuned to the shift in orientation that large, modern buildings had brought to the city. "As buildings increase in height, so the proportions change, and, instead of horizontal lines being the governing factor in design, vertical lines become the natural development," he observed. "This is clearly illustrated in the modern skyscrapers of America."

Shanghai's remarkable building boom continued even when the Great Depression brought growth to a halt in America and Europe; it didn't stop until the Second World War. In 1935 *Fortune* magazine reported Shanghai's seeming immunity from economic disaster with mystification. "Nationalism and Westernization have released new forces that were not present in 1860 or even in 1927. But neither of these explanations can account for the orgy of building, the fantastic piling of wealth upon wealth that came to Shanghai during the depression." In fact, the reasons for wealth were obvious. There were copious profits for traders who controlled the flow of goods between the West and the interior of China, as well as a burgeoning new trade on the back streets of the Bund.

Opium was the lifeblood of Shanghai's prolific underworld. The Green Gang, a complex organism spawned by what was left of feudal warlords of the Qing dynasty (which had been overthrown in 1912), established a monopoly on illicit trade about the time the Hongkong and Shanghai Bank opened its palatial headquarters. Organized crime found Shanghai especially fertile territory, as the various jurisdictions in the French, International, and Chinese zones made law enforcement almost useless. "For a uniformed member of the force to train on a Chinese suspect near Chinese territory is," wrote a British police officer, "quite hopeless."

The flesh trade brought nearly as much money as opium and was centered on side streets not far from the boulevards. "Massage parlors" were ubiquitous, many of them staffed by Russian girls, some of noble lineage and some less so. Just behind the Bund, a stretch of Kiangse Road known as "the Line"—a row of two- and three-story brick bordellos—catered to a Western clientele. Other shady or illicit activities were also conducted fairly openly. Arms dealers had the run of the place, particularly after a 1919 arms embargo brought every gunrunner in China to Shanghai's settlements, where the laws were easily circumvented. Heedless young men with money could live there in splendor, and the whiff of illegality was no bar to social cachet. They frequented places like the glass-ceilinged dining

room at the Astor Hotel, Shanghai's most stylish hostelry when it opened on the Bund in 1903. (It was designed by Atkinson & Dallas, a local firm.) One journalist described such a businessman as "a well-groomed American with a Stutz roadster and fat expense account who sold tommy guns between cocktails."

Even more innocent pastimes had a sensational aspect. The many theaters and ballrooms built in the International Settlement during the Jazz Age were designed to be as eye-catching as their entertainment was flamboyant. Over-the-top spectacles included the true story recounted in J. G. Ballard's *Empire of the Sun:* For the premiere of *The Hunchback of Notre Dame,* the cinema's promoter had the walkway lined with dwarfs and hunchbacks recruited from the back alleys of Shanghai and dressed in period costume.

Just as it fueled the pursuit of pleasure, prosperity fueled the city's growth. "If, at any time during the Coolidge prosperity," wrote *Fortune,* "you had taken your money out of American stocks and transferred it to Shanghai in the form of real-estate investments, you would have trebled it in seven years." Not bad for a period when more Wall Street investors were leaping from skyscrapers than building them. The personification of Shanghai's prosperity at the time was Sir Victor Sassoon, an Iraqi-born Englishman who was the city's leading investor and real estate developer. He led the high life of Champagne parties and horse racing, and the luxurious but streamlined buildings he built are lasting evidence of that glittery era.

Shanghai Custom House
PALMER AND TURNER, 1928
The Custom House is a symbol of Shanghai's semicolonial days, when the English and other European powers controlled trade through China's most important port. The reinforced concrete building has a granite facade, notable for its expense as compared to brick. Also noteworthy was the concrete slab foundation, engineered so that the portion beneath the clock tower would settle uniformly with the rest of the building.

Sassoon House (now Peace Hotel)
PALMER AND TURNER, 1929
Sassoon House, the crown jewel of Sir Victor Sassoon's real estate empire, included the Cathay Hotel—the epicenter of Shanghai high life, as orchestrated by one of the city's suavest playboys. The building, known today as the Peace Hotel, remains an exemplar of modernity, with its classic proportions and streamlined profile. Its distinctive copper-clad roof remains a beacon along the Bund.

The center of Sir Victor's operations was Sassoon House, which opened on the Bund at Nanjing Road in 1929. It contained the Cathay Hotel—*the* place to stay in Shanghai at the time. (It has operated since the 1950s as the Peace Hotel.) Sassoon House and the Cathay became the talk of bons vivants worldwide; Noël Coward even wrote the first draft of *Private Lives* in one of its suites. George Wilson designed it with Palmer and Turner, at last having the opportunity to build the sleek and modern skyscraper he had long imagined. Wilson, an active member of Shanghai's social set, had had many chances to bend Sir Victor's ear about modern architecture and by about 1927 had convinced him to take the next step toward it.

Twelve stories high, Sassoon House was the picture of rich modernity inside and out. Construction was in ferro cement, lighter than true stone and therefore easier on swampy foundations. Flat surfaces, vertical lines, and virtually no applied ornament gave the exterior an up-to-date profile. It was capped by a pyramid, a fashionable device of the day made popular by Howard Carter's sensational 1922 discovery of King Tut's tomb. The Cathay's interiors featured diverse themes, from rooms done in the Chinese style to an "Indian Suite," with pointed arches and arabesques, and a Jacobean design with medieval English trappings. The decor was rich but executed with the flowing space and spareness that made it as chic and contemporary as it was fascinating—like the guests who stayed there.

The Cathay of this period may be best remembered for the parties Sir Victor threw in the eleventh-floor ballrooms. One frequently chronicled soirée was a "shipwreck fancy dress ball" whose guests were asked to dress as if they had just taken to the lifeboats. The lifeboat metaphor might have been poignant, given the battles—Chinese versus Chinese, as well as Chinese versus Japanese—that

Metropole Hotel
PALMER AND TURNER, 1930
The Metropole Hotel is one of four curved edifices that form an architectural ring around the intersection of Fuzhou and Jiangxi roads, two blocks from the Bund. The modern building, with its streamlined exterior and setbacks, has stood the test of time.

Grosvenor House
PALMER AND TURNER, 1931
Another property in Sir Victor Sassoon's real estate empire, the Grosvenor (now the Jin Jiang Hotel) exuded Art Deco–style luxury inside and out.

were approaching the outskirts of Shanghai, but no sense of foreboding intruded to ruin the party spirit. The prize for best costume went to a couple wrapped up in one shower curtain. They had been showering, they said, when the ship's alarm sounded.

For some foreign residents, a haze of opium further masked the larger world's concerns. "Though I had always wanted to be an opium addict, I can't claim that was the reason I went to China," deadpanned journalist Emily Hahn, a frequent guest at Sir Victor's parties. Her drug habit (later conquered) developed simultaneously with Sino-Japanese hostilities and inured her to them, as she candidly explained: "Shells fell all around our little island of safety, and sometimes missed their mark and bounced inside it. . . . The war didn't bother me too much. I soon got used to the idea of it. Opium went up in price—that was all that mattered."

Yet the mounting tensions could not be ignored forever. With war surrounding Shanghai, land prices soared. "The settlement became a sanctuary for discredited politicians and warlords anxious to protect their lives and fortunes," wrote Stanley Jackson, Sir Victor's biographer. Unprecedented demand for accommodations spurred Sir Victor to follow his Cathay Hotel with the Metropole, Embankment House, Hamilton House, and others. Between about 1928 and 1935 he built one thousand rooms and suites for long- and short-term rental. The swiftness with which they went up was as important as their number: Sir Victor was racing against war and economic collapse to make a profit on the projects. The need to build quickly dovetailed with the unadorned, sparsely detailed modernism he now favored.

The beginning of the end came with a shock in the summer of 1937. In July, after years of conflict, Japan invaded China and the Second Sino-Japanese War began in earnest, though it would be four more years before the occupation extended into Shanghai's foreign concessions. On August 14, 1937, "Bloody Saturday," Chinese aircraft set out to attack a Japanese warship moored in Shanghai's harbor. Pilots erred and the bombs fell on the Bund. Officially, 729 people died, including American tourists and peasant refugees packed into the neighborhood. The Palace Hotel, across Nanjing Road from the Cathay, took a direct hit. The Cathay itself sustained glancing blows and, days later, the boarded-up building was a beehive. Stanley Jackson wrote, "On the third floor of Sassoon House, the company's real estate department was being flooded with inquiries for apartments, offices, shops, and godown [warehouse] space at almost any price."

Bank of China Building
PALMER AND TURNER, 1937
The Bank of China was originally designed as an Art Deco skyscraper that would have been Shanghai's tallest building. Sir Victor Sassoon vetoed the plan, ensuring that his neighboring Sassoon House retained that distinction. Serendipitously, the bank's redesign included Chinese touches, such as punched windows and an upturned cornice, that rendered it one of the Bund's most notable buildings.

That same, ominous year, the elegant, starkly modernist Bank of China building was completed next door to the Cathay, topping off just a few feet below the hotel's pyramidal Art Deco roof. Legend has it that Sir Victor had seen to it that no building in the area could rise higher than his own, preventing the bank from reaching thirty-four stories as planned. In fact, economic prudence may have guided the bank's decision to scale back. Given the worldwide depression and the Japanese occupation, it was remarkable that the building got built at all.

The Bank of China stood firmly in two worlds, traditional Chinese and modern Western finance. It had been a public-private institution until 1928, when the newly established Nationalist government founded a central bank under its full control. At that point the Bank of China shifted its focus from government functions to commercial ones—private deposits, factory loans, and foreign exchange—and moved from Beijing to Shanghai.

Its president, Zhang Gongquan, was known for a management style inspired by the tenets of Confucius. Zhang strove for the traditional Chinese balance between the vitality of the individual and the power of group objectives. Leading employees by invoking self-improvement, a Confucian concept, he emphasized the necessity of "proper spirit and attitudes," as the bank's fortunes rested on competence, integrity, and all-embracing company goals. In 1931–32—when escalating hostilities with Japan and enormous investment in high-risk bonds created turmoil in Shanghai's financial markets—Zhang removed the Bank of China from the overheated industrial economy and invested in the hinterlands. He successfully opened channels and made loans to poor peasant families.

Just as Zhang proved how modern management was compatible with Chinese thought, the new Bank of China building demonstrated the similarities between modern design and the traditions of the East. The architect, as for almost every other building on the Bund, was Palmer and Turner, but the chief designer was a Chinese, Lu Qionshou, chosen by the client. He imbued a design for a streamlined skyscraper with local flavor, adding windows incised like traditional carvings and a slightly upturned cornice.

Four years after the Bank of China's completion, the Japanese attacked Pearl Harbor, drawing the war in China into the greater Second World War and definitively ending Shanghai's golden age. The city's foreign residents were no longer immune to the strife; Japanese troops occupied and decimated the International Settlement. With Japan's defeat in 1945, China emerged nominally victorious but economically devastated and on the brink of civil war. The Communists gained power throughout the 1940s, ultimately securing control of the mainland, the establishment of the People's Republic of China in 1949, and the Nationalists' retreat to Taiwan. Any lingering foreigners left soon after. With Communist rule came a cessation of private investment—and a curtailment of thoughtful architecture—that would last some thirty years.

But even though architecture, as a creative art, was suppressed, the Bund survived.

Politicians had for decades reminded the Shanghainese that the Bund symbolized colonialism and humiliation, and its European-style temples of finance stoked the ire of Cultural Revolutionaries. But shortly after the so-called Communist liberation in 1949, the Shanghai municipal government took up in the old Hongkong and Shanghai Bank, saving it from wreckage and pillage by student cadres.

The Bund even survived the most recent revolution, the real estate explosion that flattened most of old Shanghai and rebuilt it as a vision of the twenty-first century. "To the average Chinese property speculator, history truly is bunk," wrote *The Economist* magazine in 1994. But the Bund's allure to travelers promising investment from abroad helped it beat back the relentless forces of real estate development. Preservation efforts were spearheaded by urban planners from Tongji University. They knew that saving much of Shanghai was futile, but the Bund had the advantage of imposing design. "Its elegant riverside outline is the symbol of Shanghai," a planning report stated. "Not native as it is, it represents the distinctive style of an international metropolis in the east of the world, reflecting the confluence and incorporation of Chinese and foreign cultures."

The result of the planners' efforts was the formal establishment by the mid-1990s of one of Shanghai's first historical preservation zones. New regulations prohibited demolition, and the state poured money into rehabilitating the Peace Hotel, the Hongkong and Shanghai Bank, and other projects. But the limits of the approach were quickly apparent, as new high-rise construction right at the periphery of the preservation zone shadowed the historic core.

A prime example was the Jiushi Corporation Headquarters, which was built in 2001 just beyond the Bund and within a few blocks of the old Chinese city.

Fortunately, Jiushi, by the London-based architect Norman Foster, features an unusually restrained exterior, reflecting the architect's regard for the neighborhood's historic fabric. Still, it towers forty stories above the ground and, even with its quiet profile, demonstrates the difficulty of blending the charms of old Shanghai with anything new. Another illustration of that uneasy mix is the 2002 Bund Center, a hotel and office complex whose controversial crown is conspicuous amid the Bund's staid, older structures. (The architect, John Portman, later disavowed the crown, which he claimed the developer ordered against his will.)

Custom House and Bund Center
Shanghai's history of change is etched across its skyline, with some startling juxtapositions. The neoclassical Custom House stands near the pineapple-crowned Bund Center, built by Atlanta's John Portman & Associates in 2002.

Jiushi Corporation Headquarters
FOSTER + PARTNERS, 2001
Jiushi's location between the Bund and the old Chinese city makes for a dramatic contrast of old and new Shanghai. Although architect Norman Foster designed a quiet tower—as unobtrusive as forty stories can be—it's a jarring backdrop to the low-scale, vintage buildings around it. Development turned elsewhere after its completion, in part to preserve the city's oldest sections.

Jiushi Corporation Headquarters
The tower not only offered expansive views; it also set new environmental standards for Shanghai, according to the architects. Among its innovations was a triple-skin ventilated glazing system, which allows the maximum amount of light to penetrate the interior while preventing heat from building up.

Stepped-back floor plates create light-filled interior terraces—ideal settings for business meetings or simply for marveling at the view clear across the river.

As new buildings encroached, the Bund itself began to change—not through the razing and rebuilding that characterized so much of the city's development, but through restoration. Shanghai reached a preservation milestone in 2004 with the renovation and reopening of George Wilson's first project on the Bund, the 1914 Union Assurance building. Three on the Bund, as it was renamed, was filled with luxury-goods stores and pricey restaurants that catered as little to the average Chinese as businesses on the Bund had done at the turn of the previous century. But the former insurance company headquarters, clad in beaux arts ornament, was particularly well suited to being remade into a chic emporium.

Leading this transformation was Handel Lee, a Taiwanese-born, American-trained lawyer and art collector. After arriving in Beijing in 1991 to practice law, he opened a restaurant and art gallery. Then, while seeking a location for a new gallery of contemporary art, he met the investors who held the lease to Union Assurance. Lee understood the commercial potential of historic architecture, having lived in Washington, D.C., and sold the idea to the leaseholders. Lee then hired the firm of Michael Graves, who had attained fame in America's postmodern era, and charged it with recapturing the swank luxury of Shanghai's golden age. The firm remade the interior into a series of conspicuously rich open spaces, made possible largely by the building's original steel frame. Stores were carved out of the first floors, with dazzling destination restaurants stacked above. Lavish natural materials—silk, velvet, a forest of copper and brass leaf, and abundant marble—connected the opulent past to the present.

But unlike the old Shanghai Club or Victor Sassoon's exclusive parties, the restaurants, however chic, aren't insulated from the outside world. Thomas Rowe, the project's lead architect, explained that sophisticated systems dim the lighting as evening progresses, highlighting the city beyond the windows, where the lights of Pudong's brash skyline flicker like a pinball machine. It is a view that can be seen, from varying perspectives, by elite restaurant patrons and the average Shanghainese alike: a view of the future.

Union Assurance Building (now Three on the Bund)
PALMER AND TURNER, 1914
The Union Assurance Building (above, right) was a modern structure in antique guise. Inside, the building's steel frame allowed for flexible configurations, with commercial uses on the lower floors and residential above. That adaptability allowed for the building's transformation almost ninety years later into a chic emporium called Three on the Bund.

Jean Georges, Three on the Bund
MICHAEL GRAVES & ASSOCIATES, 2004
The entrance to the restaurant Jean Georges (right) is on the fourth floor of Three on the Bund. A decorative grid of marble frames copper-leaf panels.

Atrium, Three on the Bund
MICHAEL GRAVES & ASSOCIATES, 2004
The interior of the 1914 Union Assurance Building was entirely remade into a luxuriously modern setting for upscale dining and shopping. A dramatic atrium (opposite) soars toward the light and provides peeks into the activity at several restaurants.

AS LATE AS 1990 the world beyond China was talking more or less in unison about the "chimera" of Chinese capitalism, agreeing that a country with a government so despotic hardly made a good investment. Economists wrote cautionary papers. The press carried stories of Western businesses foundering in China. American Motors entered a partnership in China, and its managers, angered by the ensuing difficulties, expressed the common Western view: The Chinese objective was simply to grab as much Western technology as possible and then divorce those who had brought it.

Western architects faced similar deterrents to working in China: language barriers, clients' failure to pay, and, in a country where intellectual property rights were routinely violated, a suspicion that nonbinding design competitions served as a way to steal ideas. The competition process itself was costly, and the results were capricious. Still, the potential was tempting. A Toronto firm, Webb Zerafa Menkes Housden (WZMH), had participated in one of the earliest Shanghai design competitions, but no building ever came of it. Even so, in 1991, when WZMH was invited to compete for another project, the firm found the prospects so intriguing that it set aside its doubts and decided to take part.

The Shanghai Securities Exchange would be China's nerve center for private investment and a focal point of Lujiazui, Pudong's new financial district. WZMH's architect Brian Andrew found the program brief conservative, specifying a forty-story tower with offices and a pedestal or base containing a trading room. It included a stern warning that any deviation from those specifications would result in disqualification. So Andrew and WZMH adhered to the instructions—although, in Andrew's experience, competitions were usually won by breaking the rules—but offered a somewhat unpredictable design: Their scheme placed the pedestal to the side, not underneath the glass tower, adding exterior interest and, more important, allowing for a larger span of columnless trading-room space. WZMH was awarded the commission.

Unexpectedly—especially given the warning to follow the explicit guidelines—the client immediately requested an entirely new design. The client was Shanghai Puly Real Estate, a semiprivate development company. Formally working on behalf of the government, which was financing the stock exchange, Shanghai Puly also had a sharp entrepreneurial side. "They seemed aggressive," Andrew said. "They reminded me of New Yorkers."

Lujiazui skyline
Pudong is a vast district covering 202 square miles, but its densest cluster is the Lujiazui financial district. About a mile square, Lujiazui contains some seventy major buildings. Among the most prominent are (from left to right) Bank of Shanghai (Kenzo Tange, 2005), Bocom Financial Towers (ABB Architekten, 2002), Bank of China Tower (Nikken Sekkei, 2000), and Jin Mao Tower (Adrian Smith of Skidmore Owings and Merrill, 1999).

Shanghai Securities Exchange
WEBB ZERAFA MENKES HOUSDEN, 1997
The stock exchange's interior required a large trading room but had no need for a soaring tower, which led to its distinctive bridgelike form. Even after a forest of buildings grew tall around it, the building remains a landmark.

X-braces had become a familiar modernist device since diagonal steel trusses were first used to support Chicago's John Hancock Building in 1968.

The trading room's vast clear-span space, uninterrupted by internal supports, is made possible by the building's prominent exoskeleton.

Keenly ambitious for Lujiazui and Pudong, the developers were concerned that a single forty-story office tower would soon be lost amid the fast-growing city's ever-taller buildings. They wanted their building to stand up over time. Newly inspired, Andrew came up with the "gateway" design that was completed in 1997. Its two vertical sections are connected beneath by a pedestal and above by another horizontal—a radical profile, though it echoes the Grande Arche at La Défense, the Paris business district, and a well-known unbuilt design for Tokyo's city hall. The form provided a large-span trading room on the lower floors and ample office space above. At least as important was the design's symbolic impact. "We described it as a gateway," Andrew said. "That was a word that worked and connected—the gateway or bridge to the future and to the past."

The metaphor was an important component of the design, though the building's symbolism never overshadowed its function. "Seeing buildings in symbolic terms is more common in Asia and especially in China than in the West," Andrew said. "In North America you'd have to justify something like this on a completely pragmatic level." Despite his understanding of the role of symbolism in Chinese architecture, Andrew was surprised during a visit to the stock exchange to overhear a guide explaining to a group of tourists that its architect was inspired above all by the form of ancient Chinese coins, typically round with a square hole in the middle. Andrew took it as a reminder that a building's symbolism can evolve over the years.

Pudong, before and after development

Before Beijing gave its blessing to Shanghai's development, Pudong was little more than rice fields, small factories, and concrete buildings for workers, with few amenities besides the view of the Bund. In the 1990s it became the focus of the most intense urban growth the world had ever known. Photos taken at the confluence of the Huangpu River and Suzhou Creek show the vast change between 1980 (opposite, top) and the late 1990s (opposite, bottom).

Pudong apartments

The master plans for Pudong that were submitted by an international panel of experts were largely disregarded. The ad hoc approach that ensued resulted in housing—such as the apartment buildings (below) seen from Jin Mao Tower—placed amid Lujiazui's commercial skyscrapers.

The developers of the stock exchange were not alone in their aspirations for Pudong. In fact, talk of developing Pudong had begun as long ago as the 1920s, when the Nationalist Chinese leader Sun Yat-sen proposed the broad alluvial flats opposite the Bund's colonial riverfront for Shanghai's future growth. War, then the Cultural Revolution, interrupted the realization of any such plans, and the area remained a vast expanse of rice paddies and low-rise concrete buildings.

Still, there were signs of change. A new subway line was begun in 1986, including two stops in Pudong, and construction of the Oriental Pearl Television Tower got under way soon thereafter. But the turning point for Pudong was Mayor Zhu Ronghi's 1991 fact-finding trip to Paris. At a meeting with members of France's architecture and urban planning establishment, Zhu said he rejected the "free-wheeling" style of American cities, preferring a strict plan for Pudong, which he sought to model after La Défense, the modern business zone within sight of, but separate from, Paris. The French were both honored by the mayor's view and aware that it could lead to their playing an important role in Shanghai's future. In their earliest discussions, Zhu and his delegation explained that Pudong's development would center on a financial hub near the river, Lujiazui, a square-mile area where nearly forty million square feet of commercial space would be constructed as soon as possible. The French experts, including Joseph Belmont, minister of public architecture, suggested that a well-publicized international competition would help advance such ambitious plans—and that the involvement of world-famous architects would be a good way to attract investors' attention.

Shanghai officials were concerned that the winner of a high-profile competition would demand more control than the city was willing to cede—an objection the French defused by suggesting an international "consultation." Zhu (whose power was rising; he was about to move to Beijing as vice prime minister) had often emphasized the importance of foreign consultants in China, which had fallen well behind the rest of the developed world. He said, "outsiders sometimes have greater wisdom because they can look at things from the outside," and took to calling his consultants "foreign monks."

Zhu and Belmont devised an unusual selection process for the consultation, nominating two architects from each of four countries, then choosing one from each. Thus Richard Rogers was selected over Norman Foster to represent England; Dominique Perrault over Jean Nouvel, France; Massimiliano Fuksas over Renzo Piano, Italy; and Toyo Ito over Kazuo Shinahara, Japan. None had significant experience in China, but that was not considered a drawback. Zhu said Shanghai needed "the shock of the new" to rouse it from somnambulism.

A year later, after several visits to Shanghai, the four architects presented plans. Massimiliano Fuksas's was arguably the one most connected to local history, albeit abstractly. His plan took on a circular form with a wide canal running through, references to the wall surrounding medieval Shanghai and the creeks that coursed through the old city. He also proposed successive levels of density, with the tallest buildings clustered in the center and progressively shorter buildings in the outer rings of the circle. To combat the automotive traffic plaguing most large cities, Fuksas pushed most traffic toward the periphery, keeping the busy center largely absent of cars. This central element of the plan did not resonate with the Chinese overseeing the project. "We love our cars," a planning official told the architect. At another point a local official announced that Shanghai regarded bicycle traffic as excessive, and any usable city plan should seek to curtail it.

The other three architects' plans likewise attempted to control density and leave space for the city to live and breathe. After a nonbinding jury process, Richard Rogers's entry was cited as the "winner." His circular plan, suggestive of an English garden city, was circumscribed by a series of ring roads, within which were divisions creating several distinct quarters, each with its own high-rises, houses, and parks. Rogers's triumph was hollow, however, as the municipal government proceeded instead with a plan devised by the Shanghai Planning Institute, a scheme reminiscent of America's late nineteenth-century City Beautiful movement. It had a wide axial boulevard lined by major buildings and parks, better suited to a ceremonial center than a financial one.

By this time, however, it was clear that Pudong's development was never going to adhere to a strict urban plan; construction sites began appearing long before one could be implemented. Real estate investors were coming from Taiwan, Hong Kong, and Chinese communities in the United States and other countries, and the Shanghai government, eager to oblige, let them build where they liked. Attracting investment had been the purpose of the international consultation, after all, and district officials (perhaps swayed by the usual measure of corruption) were not inclined to interfere with signed, paid-for property leases.

In the absence of urban planning, the buildings that rose were as capricious in their design as they were in their site selection. Pudong's building boom was unfortunately coincident with the last gasps of the postmodern style in the West. The result was "a riot of wild architectural hats—levitating, spiky, jagged, like the jaws of a techno-monster," wrote Christopher Choa, an American architect working in Shanghai, in a 2004 *Time* magazine article.

The goulash of exaggerated designs was only exacerbated by the design competitions usually required by law for commissions of any size. The decisions of juries—often made up of academics and practicing professionals—were not binding; developers who didn't like the outcome could ask for a second round or otherwise fix the result to suit. And in Shanghai, with its taste for unique architectural statements, competitions were especially likely to spawn designs that shout for attention. As American architect Adrian Smith put it, "They are a good way to get over-the-top architecture."

Lujiaziu skyscrapers
Of all of the skyscrapers that rose in Pudong in the 1990s, the two-towered China Insurance (Webb Zerafa Menkes Housden, 1999) may take postmodernism to its farthest extreme. Its rounded corners and antennalike needles recall science fiction imagery of the 1920s. The green-tinted China Merchants Tower (Simon Kwan & Associates, 1995) suggests a robot of midcentury vintage.

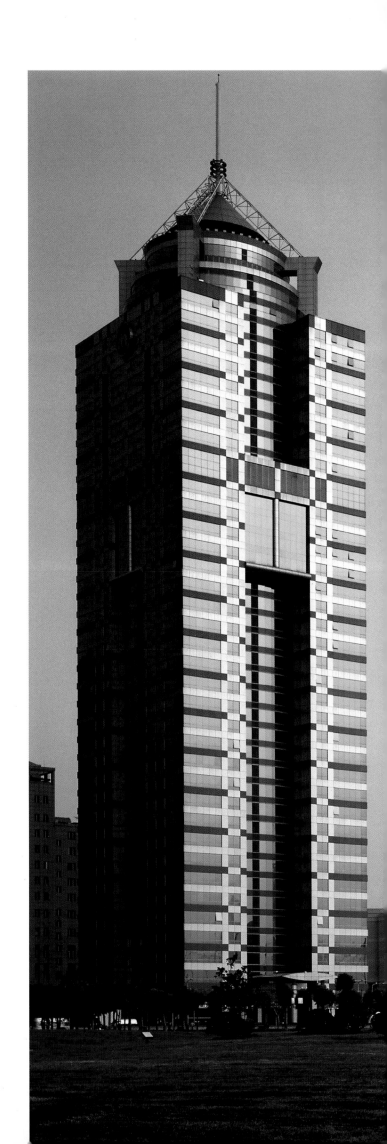

King Tower
TAO HO, 1996
King Tower has touches of the familiar—namely San Francisco's Transamerica Pyramid—but altogether is a massive assembly of seemingly disparate parts.

An example is King Tower, which at thirty-eight stories was Pudong's tallest building when it was completed in 1996. The government's competition yielded a design that is hard not to notice. It is the work of Hong Kong architect Tao Ho, who studied at Harvard in the 1960s and while there was personal assistant to Walter Gropius, the architect who founded the Bauhaus. But little about King Tower suggests the influence of Gropius's "integrated industrial arts." The form bears a caricatured resemblance to the Transamerica Pyramid of San Francisco, which like the King Tower houses insurance companies. Beyond that, it's no more than a postmodern pastiche of promiscuous origin.

Other flamboyant buildings quickly rose in Pudong in the 1990s, and many inspired glib labels. The new Bank of China Tower was described in *Domus*, an Italian design magazine, as "lipstick revolving out of its protective sheath." The same article bitingly sketched an unnamed building by the river, probably the Shangri-La Hotel, as "Ricardo Bofill on one side, with giant precast stone Corinthian columns, and Richard Meier's Getty Center on the other." Other structures were likened to hat pins, silos, and *The Jetsons*, the space age cartoon. It was a rococo period of postmodernism, and Shanghai's architecture typically embraced form at the expense of function. Still, some found merit in the newfangled skyline. In his generally laudatory *Time* article Christopher Choa granted that, though most of the new buildings were "just a fantastic pastiche, . . . they do serve a useful function; it's easy to get lost in a city of more than 16 million souls, and sometimes you desperately need to get a fix on an unusual shape to remember exactly where you are."

A rare masterpiece among Chinese skyscrapers of the 1990s is Jin Mao Tower, designed by Adrian Smith for Chicago-based Skidmore Owings and Merrill (SOM) and completed in 1999. In 1992, when construction was moribund in the United States, SOM, like other American firms, looked abroad, seeking an invitation to compete for Jin Mao. It was intended to be the tallest building in China, with offices on the lower floors and a hotel on the upper ones; it was also to be one of three eventual "supertall" structures (each at least eighty stories) clustered near the Huangpu River. Not everyone at SOM was high on the prospect, given the known drawbacks of Chinese design competitions. Even with a fifty thousand dollar stipend, generous by Chinese standards, competing for Jin Mao seemed like a losing proposition. But Smith, one of the firm's leading design partners at the time, volunteered to take it on.

The client was a group of mercantile companies with strong financial backing from the government in Beijing. Underscoring the importance of the project, a delegation representing the client traveled to Chicago to meet with SOM. The apparent leader of the delegation, a Mr. Zhang, explained that the building would have eighty-eight stories, as the number eight represented surpassingly good luck. The numerological significance was reinforced at a dinner in Chicago's Chinatown. By chance, eight people were seated around the table, a fact Zhang noted with pleasure. After the meal, when he opened his fortune cookie, all the numbers listed on its message—provided to suggest lottery picks—were multiples of eight. Smith commented on the auspicious omens for SOM.

Using the number as his main guide, Smith tried a skyscraper with eight sections of eleven stories, then eleven sections of eight, but these looked static and uninteresting on paper. Eventually he and his team came up with a scheme that began at ground level with sixteen stories. Next came a stack, slightly set back, of fourteen stories, which was sixteen reduced by one-eighth. The formula (with some rounding off) continued with successive stacks until the last level, a single story, reached the propitious total of eighty-eight. Also critical was the tower's "historicist design using modern technologies," as Smith put it. Its pagodalike profile was intricately decorated with a network of stainless steel mullions that screened the building's skin. "Competitions are won and lost on the idea," said Smith. In this case, the idea won.

Jin Mao Tower
SKIDMORE OWINGS AND MERRILL WITH ADRIAN SMITH, DESIGN PRINCIPAL, 1999
At eighty-eight stories, Jin Mao was the tallest building in China when built. It's likely to remain so until the completion of the neighboring World Financial Center in about 2008. Its profile evokes the Chinese pagoda, which the architect called "one of the world's first forms of man-made skyscrapers."

Jin Mao's exterior is granite, stainless steel, aluminum, and glass. The metal grillwork gleams with modernity but also expresses the building's contextualism, recalling the upturned eaves and handmade construction of China's traditional architecture.

Jin Mao Tower
The tower's four-level atrium is a light-filled retail and entertainment complex. It is crossed by a zigzag bridge, a modern reference to the one in Yu Yuan Gardens.

The spiral is a recurring motif at Jin Mao. In Chinese thought it suggests the universe and eternity. It is seen on a grand scale in the building's hotel atrium, which rises thirty-one stories (opposite).

Another Western architect to obtain major commissions in Shanghai, Paul Andreu of France, succeeded by rejecting flashy futuristic notions and submitting designs much like those he would undertake elsewhere. Andreu, an archetypal modern architect—innovative with technology and determined to wed evocative form to complicated function—made his name as the principal designer of Charles de Gaulle Airport outside Paris. His challenge for Shanghai Pudong International Airport was not just to create a state-of-the-art facility but to infuse it with symbolism.

Andreu had little experience with Asian culture prior to 1996, when he sought the commission for the airport's first phase, and his initial encounters with the jury in Shanghai were not encouraging. His proposal was notable for the green space and lakes surrounding the terminal. The first jury, made up of engineers and planning officials, reviewed Andreu's drawings with pained body language, and their few questions suggested that they regarded the parkland as a waste of space. In his second presentation, to a panel of politicians whose decision would be final, Andreu defended the green space as indispensable. Aware that Chinese leaders were eager to improve their image as world-class polluters, he began by saying that any airport is its city's first opportunity to make an impression on visitors. Peaceful lakes and lush green space would allow a modern airport to be integrated into the natural environment.

The curving roof line suggested wings, but Andreu was dismissive of avian imagery as the immense project's motivating idea. Understanding the importance of the metaphysical in Chinese buildings, he encouraged the jury to see beyond the winglike silhouette, explaining that he "thought of an airport as a place where you pass from one place to another, from train to plane, from the earth to the sky." The bluish tint in the glass, discernible mostly at night, would

reinforce the connection to the sky—a point Andreu underscored with a poem, translated from the French, about the "azure sky" in an enchanted place. "Many international juries are afraid of this kind of thing," Andreu said. "They think you are just trying to make fools of them." Not in China. The presentation yielded a richer dialogue with a potential client, a major commission, and a new nickname, "The Poet," as the Chinese call Andreu.

More Chinese commissions subsequently came his way. The Oriental Arts Center in Pudong was completed in 2004, and the National Theater in Beijing— controversial for its prominent location beside the Great Hall of the People—in 2006. Along with the airport, they quickly become icons, and the Chinese cast Andreu in the role of master builder. (The collapse of a terminal at Charles de Gaulle in 2003 and the fact that two of the four people killed were Chinese were painful twists for the architect and his Chinese clients.)

Shanghai Pudong International Airport
PAUL ANDREU, 1999
Although Andreu insisted that function, not symbolism, drove his design, he likened the airport's exterior form to "the petals of a flower, the wings of a bird, or the widening ripples formed by the breeze on the water."

Shanghai Pudong International Airport
The cables and vertical supports that hold the terminal's metal roof aloft bestow a sense of weightlessness upon the interior (opposite).

Oriental Arts Center
PAUL ANDREU, 2004
Pudong's primary concert hall takes the form of five unequal "lobes," each dedicated to a distinct function, including performance, administration, exhibition, and retail. The largest of the center's three concert halls seats nearly two thousand and unmistakably reflects the exterior's orchidlike form.

Century Avenue
PLAN BY ARTE CHARPENTIER, LANDSCAPE BY
PHILIPPE THÉBAUD, 1999
Although construction in Pudong preceded any coordinated planning effort, Century Avenue effectively connected the pieces that were already in place as well as those under development, helping to give order to the district and guide future development along its axis.

The architects imposed a uniform design on Century Avenue's lighting and street furniture, underscoring the boulevard's image as a unifier of the sometimes wildly disparate elements along its five-mile course.

With French landscape architect Philippe Thébaud the Charpentier firm laid out a series of gardens along Century Avenue. Treillage and enclosures were among the features meant "to invite people to stroll, take their time, engage in meditation," according to Pierre Clément, Jean-Marie Charpentier's partner and planning expert.

Century Avenue

ARTE CHARPENTIER, 1999

Seeking a human scale for a miles-long boulevard, Arte Charpentier lined Century Avenue with landscaping and punctuated it with intersections, rather than create an expressway. However, its great width—328 feet—presents a challenge to pedestrians hoping to cross.

Another Pudong commission of the 1990s, the Shanghai Science and Technology Museum was regarded by government officials as vitally important for both its position near the end of Pudong's main thoroughfare, Century Avenue, and its content, China's technological skill. The Baltimore-based firm RTKL was invited to compete, and the task of designing the entry went to Chinese-born Liu Xiaoguang, who worked in the firm's Los Angeles office. Liu was wary of juries' tendency, especially marked in Pudong, to value meaningless form over function. "Here," he said, "everyone wants to create a landmark."

Liu had no intention of losing the commission by neglecting the Chinese predilection for symbolic form, but his priority was to create a functional design for a modern museum. His scheme took shape around a sweeping semicircular roof line, which was meant to reflect a hybrid of the Western notion of linear prog-

ress and the Chinese idea of a spiral-shaped universe. Other elements, notably a geodesic globe penetrating the roof from below, had symbolic content as well as architectonic function, centering and anchoring the composition as a whole.

Liu's asymmetrical scheme won the competition, but RTKL sensed that politics could sink its commission. Rumors were that a Paris firm was lobbying strenuously for the museum job, and ties between Pudong and the French were still very strong. So Liu and his partners applied some muscle of their own, appealing through intermediaries to officials in Washington, D.C. When President Bill Clinton visited China in June 1998, he met with the mayor of Shanghai to jointly announce that RTKL would design the prestigious new museum. Having the leader of the Western world declare the result as a fait accompli was perhaps the surest way to overcome the vagaries of Chinese architectural competitions.

Shanghai Science and Technology Museum
RTKL, 2001
The dazzling design of the $200 million museum landed it on a list of China's best buildings, selected by Chinese architects and planners at a 2003 convention.

Shanghai Science and Technology Museum
The upward curve of the museum's roof has more symbolic than functional significance. To the designer, Liu Xiaoguang of RTKL, it is part of a spiral representing the trajectory of scientific history and discovery. The glass globe symbolizes the yolk of an egg, or the origin of life.

Shanghai Science and Technology Museum
The geodesic globe serves as the entrance to the museum, which has more space than its exhibits could initially fill.

General Motors Building
ARTE CHARPENTIER, 2004

General Motors Shanghai was created in 1997, a joint venture of the Detroit automaker and the state-owned Shanghai Automotive Industry Corporation. The first years were marked by growing pains, as American and Chinese management styles clashed. But by the time G.M.'s new headquarters opened on Century Avenue, Chinese car ownership was growing and the company was prospering.

The openwork roof recalls modernist classics like Skidmore Owings and Merrill's Finnish Pavilion at the 1939 New York World's Fair. The design is horizontal, but the void in the overhang opens to infinite verticality.

The architects developed a public green space along the G.M. headquarters's south side, where the sun would encourage plants and cheer pedestrians. With its human scale and landscaping, the G.M. Building resists the skyscrapers' invasion of Pudong. It is set along a comparatively low-rise section of Century Avenue.

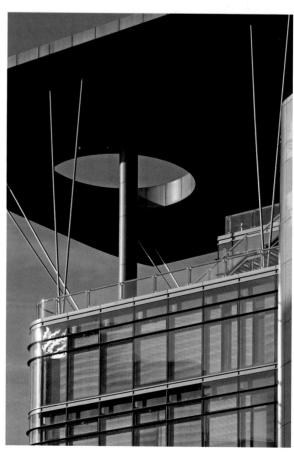

Politics and arbitrary design competitions may always play an important role in Shanghai's development, and architecture's symbolism will likely continue to have greater prominence in China than in the West. However, recent buildings indicate that, after years of unbridled excess, Pudong's architecture has matured. Once, Shanghai developers endlessly repeated that they wanted something "unique, unique, and more unique," said Jim Goettsch of Chicago's Goettsch Partners. But Goettsch's commission for Shanghai's diamond exchange, expected to be completed by 2009, suggests that clients now understand that function must drive form, the basic tenet of modernism.

Goettsch's client for Lujiazui Diamond Tower, rising on a site near the end of Century Avenue, is a consortium of Chinese diamond merchants. Their guidelines were to divide the building between exhibit space on one side and offices on the other and to eschew privileged offices—a rare vestige of egalitarianism in modern Communist China. This practical program led to a simple, strikingly modern design, with two fifteen-story sides connected by an atrium, and elevators—not private offices—placed in the corners. The fritted glass screen planned for large sections of the exterior will diffuse the light entering the building, making the diamonds for sale inside look their best. Altogether, functional elements dictated the design's aesthetic content.

Another building notable for its restrained design is the Shanghai Municipal Electric Power headquarters, completed in 2005. While the building is not bereft of decorative flourishes, it's not overwhelmed by them, either. The result is even more impressive given the extraordinarily difficult conditions the project presented to the Haipo Group, a large Shanghai firm owned by two American-trained Chinese architects. A hulking concrete core had been erected on the site by an inexperienced, underfinanced developer, who was unable to finish. Substandard floor-to-ceiling heights were already cast in concrete. Haipo's solution was to wrap a glass curtain wall around the existing core but leave an opening where floor plates were set back at every second story. That added exterior interest and also created a series of small two-story atriums running all the way up the tower's thirty stories, compensating for the low ceilings.

The gap in the skin curving around the building allowed for a series of two-story atriums, brightening the low-ceilinged interior.

Shanghai Municipal Electric Power Building
HAIPO GROUP, 2005
After a decade of frenzied construction and over-the-top design, Shanghai developed a taste for architecture driven by function and greater restraint, a trend exemplified by the electric company's headquarters. The building's one subtle element of symbolism was the bluish green glass, intended to signify harmony with the earth and the sky.

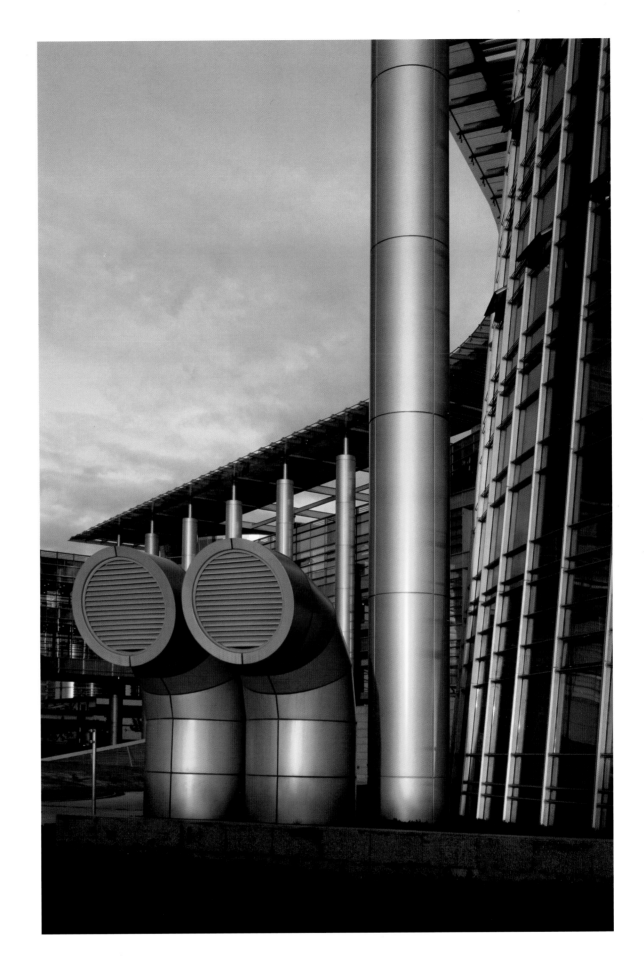

Shanghai Municipal Electric Power Building
The electric company's offices are in the tower, and a technical operations center is housed in the pedestal around it. The functional design resulted in a building of quiet refinement, with a measure of flash so as not to appear impoverished by comparison to new Shanghai's exuberant architecture.

The classic modern lines at the diamond exchange and the discerning solutions to practical challenges there and at the Shanghai Municipal Electric Power Building are evidence of Shanghai's architectural advancement. Nevertheless, Pudong still awaits the distinctive icon that would define the world's densest concentration of skyscrapers. A candidate for that title was the World Financial Center, designed by New York's Kohn Pedersen Fox, which will be Shanghai's tallest building when completed in 2008 or so. But the changes it has undergone since its 1997 groundbreaking and its long delayed construction suggest that the building's moment may have passed even before its completion.

Originally intended as not the city's but the world's tallest building, the WFC's design was innovative, with tapered walls and a great oculus at the top that were both aesthetically interesting and functional: The building would perform well in the wind, critical in so high a structure. But construction was halted, partly by the Asian financial crisis. When work resumed in 2003 the WFC's tapered profile was commonplace and buildings in other cities had surpassed its 1,614-foot height. Most unfortunately, the aperture at top was changed from a circle to a less beautiful rectangle, in response to concerns over its symbolism. The oculus was thought to resemble Japan's emblematic rising sun and—especially since the building's developer is a Japanese firm—potentially be seen as a provocation by China's historical rival. The net result is that the completion of a building whose plans were greeted with fanfare is now awaited with indifference.

The WFC's shifting fortunes demonstrate both the elusiveness of architectural distinction and how architecture's merits may only be gauged over time. It is impossible to anticipate how a structure will be regarded even ten years after its completion. A building deemed uninspired when new may eventually be embraced as strong and eternal; one that now seems laden with kitsch may someday be a much-loved part of the urban fabric. So final judgment of the rakish and peculiar buildings that rose in Pudong in the 1990s cannot yet be rendered—but surely their very excesses will be remembered as symbols of Shanghai's irrepressible optimism at the dawn of the twenty-first century.

Pudong skyline
Chen Yi Fei's 1999 sculpture, *The Sundial,* signals the end of Century Avenue. Pudong rises behind it with emphatic modernity. Flanking the sculpture are POS Tower (Pei Cobb Freed, 1999), to the left, and Shanghai Financial Tower (Langdon Wilson, 1998), to the right. At far right is the Shanghai Municipal Electric Power headquarters (Haipo Group, 2005).

BEYOND THE BUND Puxi's Blend of Old and New

WILD GROWTH in the 1990s may have transformed the rural lands of Pudong into a flashy new commercial district on the eastern shore of the Huangpu River, but Shanghai's urban core remains on the opposite bank. The sprawling city's past and present downtown, now called Puxi (literally, "west of the River"), radiates from the Bund on all three sides, encompassing the former foreign concessions.

Like Pudong, Puxi began a cycle of dramatic growth in the last years of the twentieth century, with modern skyscrapers transforming its skyline. But behind its glittering new facade it retains the diversity and vibrancy that long characterized old Shanghai. In the late nineteenth and early twentieth centuries, the foreign zones represented safe haven from warlords, insurrections, and other

Xintiandi

Xintiandi was the city's first major attempt to adapt its old structures to new uses. It transformed a low-rise *lilong* neighborhood of tightly clustered row houses into an outdoor mall of chic restaurants and shops.

turmoil besetting the country. Shanghai's population swelled with people from elsewhere in China, erasing any vestige of ethnic segregation.

Through the next decades of brittle peace and unbridled prosperity, Shanghai grew steadily, stretching away from the riverfront unimpeded by economic restraints or natural barriers. While the Bund maintained its stately European looks, no single architectural style defined the rest of the city. Brash electric lights and colorful signs adorned the commercial buildings along Nanjing Road. In the International Settlement and French Concession, ultramodern Art Deco apartments rose amid opium dens, bordellos, and snazzy ballrooms. Farther out, parklike estates in English, Spanish, and Craftsman styles dotted the countryside.

Its rich mix of cultures and languages, amusements and dangers, made Shanghai unlike any other place in China. Vividly encapsulating the amalgam of East and West was Nanjing (then Nanking) Road, which more or less bisected the International Settlement. "Along its length were pagoda-roofed goldsmiths' and silversmiths' shops, porcelain and curio dealers, and silk emporiums whose shelves spilled over with rich satins and embroideries," wrote Stella Dong in *Shanghai: The Rise and Fall of a Decadent City,* published in 2000. "Whereas in the Chinese City shopkeepers sat bare to the waist fanning their stomachs on sticky days, on Nanking Road the merchants and clerks wore long gray gowns and never rolled up their sleeves—a sign of ill-breeding—while serving customers."

The area's concentration of customers and wealth soon brought modern department stores to Nanjing Road. Two of the most important—the "Gimbels and Macy's of Shanghai," as Dong put it—were the Sincere and Wing On stores, which opened in 1917 and 1918, respectively. They offered a vivid, intoxicating blend of the Western retail experience and the Oriental bazaar, as captured by a passage from the autobiography of director Josef von Sternberg. In addition to miles of merchandise, the store he visited had "every variety of entertainment Chinese ingenuity had contrived. . . . On the first floor were gambling tables, sing-song girls, magicians, pickpockets, slot machines, fireworks." The ornate towers atop Sincere and Wing On's retail palaces drew people from a distance and define Nanjing Road's shopping district to this day.

Lively with crowds, Nanjing Road was the focal point of entertainment, social interaction, and other events animating public life. For example, in 1927, when Chiang Kai-shek's troops approached Shanghai, Nationalist flags were flown from the store windows, and populist leaflets floated down from the rooftop of Wing On. Although a nervous coalition of European troops and local warlords had erected barricades, the Nationalist army marched down Nanjing Road and took the city.

Until that point, Shanghai had been largely insulated from the instability wracking China. Warlords, Nationalists, and Communists had been struggling for control since the 1912 overthrow of the Qing dynasty had ended two thousand years of imperial rule. Now a Nationalist-Communist alliance was to come to a bloody end in the streets of Shanghai, where Chiang Kai-shek expediently joined up with some of the more ruthless local gangsters. In what became known as the Shanghai Massacre, he purged the Communists in his ranks and had Red sympathizers hunted down and executed. Over several days in April, "heads rolled into the gutters of the narrow lanes like ripe plums," as one witness described it in Dong's book.

After the massacre, a superficial normalcy returned. Tens of thousands of foreigners continued to inhabit Shanghai; business continued to boom. Shoppers thronged the department stores on Nanjing Road, while other patrons frequented the bordellos on Fuzhou Road, a couple of blocks away.

Nanjing Road, 1930s

In the early twentieth century Nanjing Road (opposite) had a measure of refinement. Primarily Chinese merchants furnished a European clientele with an array of luxury goods. The two towers in midground top the Wing On and Sincere department stores, which remain in operation.

Nanjing Road

Today part of Nanjing Road is a teeming pedestrian mall, filled with department stores, specialty shops, and restaurants. "The Chinese delight in brilliant light," as an English guidebook put it in 1920. The neon along Nanjing Road shows that they still do almost a century later.

The Mayor's Building or New City Hall
DONG DAYOU, 1934
Dong's city hall was a prominent example of a short-lived attempt to marry Western modernism with Asian traditions. It was built as part of a planned civic center, a project curtailed by the Japanese occupation in 1937.

A centralized Nationalist government was set up under Chiang Kai-shek in 1928. The modern municipal governments the fledgling republic established were in great need of urban planning and construction. Contemporary skills in those fields were lacking, so many architectural students from Shanghai and other coastal cities traveled abroad for training. Most prominent among the American colleges they attended was the University of Pennsylvania, where the school of architecture was headed by Paul Philippe Cret, a distinguished architect and a leading proponent of the beaux arts style.

Cret's design philosophy was not universally embraced in America's architectural circles; it was deplored by most modernists, who saw neoclassicism as the enemy of progress, a throwback to a previous age. Yet the training Cret provided ran deeper than Greek and Roman facades. He taught that good design was universal, not derived from *styles* as much as from an understanding of function and plan. That principle appealed to many Chinese who were seeking a national architecture and whose traditions appeared ill suited to modern growth. One of Cret's most notable students, Liang Sicheng, returned to China after graduation from Penn in 1927 and became instrumental in founding the department of architecture at Northeastern University in Mukden, Manchuria. Liang spent most of his career training a new generation of Chinese architects largely in Cret's principles.

Others returned from the West to open practices, among them Dong Dayou, a graduate of programs at Minnesota and Columbia. In 1933 Dong designed a plan for a civic center, part of a larger Shanghai development scheme ordered by the Nationalist government. The ornamental symmetry of his plan owed a debt to America's City Beautiful movement, which had itself grown out of the beaux arts, but Dong put a Chinese stamp on the details. One of the few elements of the scheme to be executed, the city hall, was an extraordinary hybrid, neoclassical in its symmetry but with an extravagant pagodalike roof—an early example of how Chinese architects, like Chinese politicians, sought to express a national identity for the modern world.

Other architects working in Shanghai followed a more emphatically modern course, largely excising historical and local influences from their designs. Among these was Robert Fan (born Fan Wenzhao), who began his education in Shanghai and early in his career designed conventional Western-style buildings with Chinese touches, such as slightly upturned eaves and ornamental brackets. Then he went to Pennsylvania, where he studied with Cret. After returning to Shanghai in 1927, Fan largely renounced traditional architecture and designed "from the inside out," not "from the outside in," as he wrote, echoing the modernist creed espoused by Frank Lloyd Wright and Walter Gropius's Bauhaus. Fan found a local clientele that included the owners of the Art Deco–style Majestic Theatre, built in 1941.

Paramount Ballroom
YANG XILIU, 1934

The Paramount was a Shanghai hot spot in the prewar years, with dance floors, a lounge, a bar, and banquet halls catering to Chinese and foreign residents alike. Chinese architects were hired to design many such buildings, while more important commissions went to Europeans. With the recent revival of interest in ballroom dancing, the Art Deco palace has been largely restored and attracts local café society and tourists.

Majestic Theatre
ROBERT FAN, 1941

The Majestic, one of the many Art Deco theaters built during Shanghai's golden age, was designed by Robert Fan, one of the city's numerous Chinese-born, American-trained architects. It was not the most luxurious theater even in its heyday, but the Majestic exemplifies the good, timeless design of the Art Deco period. It is once again a popular entertainment venue.

The foremost modern architecture of Shanghai's golden age not only ignored Chinese traditions but was designed by one of the city's many foreign residents, Laszlo Hudec, a Hungarian. After escaping from a Russian prisoner-of-war train in Siberia in 1918, Hudec—armed with a recent degree from the Royal Hungarian Technical University—quickly made himself part of Shanghai's fledgling building boom. An American architectural firm took him on, and in 1925 he went out on his own. He proved to be one of the city's most prolific architects, with more than fifty buildings to his name. His career paralleled the explosive growth of business in Shanghai, when the turmoil of war in Europe threw opportunities to Chinese industry.

Hudec's most significant client was a bank, the Joint Savings Society, whose systems were being transformed by Western practices and whose new build-

D. V. Wood residence
LASZLO HUDEC, 1938
The Wood or "Woo" house exemplifies the streamlined modern style of many Shanghai villas and apartment buildings of the 1930s. "Dr. Woo" was a successful merchant of pigments, and his house is considered among the finest examples of Art Deco architecture. Yet, interestingly, the architect built himself a Tudor mansion.

ings would reflect its new ways. Banking had a long tradition in imperial China, though most old-style banks were local in scope. The fall of the Qing dynasty took many of those institutions down with it, whereupon Chinese knowledgeable about Western banking practices—some with experience in banks on the Bund—filled the vacuum. In 1927 there were forty-eight "modern" banks in China, performing advanced functions such as foreign exchange, correspondent relations in other cities and countries, and even the issuance of paper money. One of the most prominent banks was Joint Savings, which was created in 1922 from the merger of four strong Shanghai institutions. Hudec's design for the Joint Savings headquarters, completed in 1928, was neoclassical in style, surely intended to underscore the bank's solidity with its resemblance to European institutions. But it was subtly simplified and streamlined, revealing the architect's modern impulse.

Hudec's great success came with Joint Savings's decision to build an income-producing skyscraper overlooking the racetrack at the intersection of Nanjing and Thibet roads (now People's Park). The resulting Park Hotel, which opened in 1934, was, at twenty-two stories, the tallest building in Asia for many years. At the time of its construction, when the Chinese regarded the accumulation of wealth as modern—even, according to contemporary articles, patriotic—the building's purpose, unabashed size, and streamlined style made it the picture of modernity.

Hudec began the design in 1929, shortly after visiting America, where he was impressed by New York City and its skyscrapers, both the "gothicized modern" ones and the more emphatically sleek, like the Empire State and Chrysler buildings. He especially admired the work of modernist architect Raymond Hood; in an article he referred to Hood's New York Daily News Building as "magnificent." New York's Art Deco influence can be seen in the Park Hotel's dramatic setbacks and soaring vertical lines. The dark tile on the Park's exterior also echoes the black brickwork of Hood's American Radiator Building in midtown Manhattan.

The Park Hotel made for a clear contrast with the Cathay, constructed just two years earlier a few blocks away on the Bund. Hudec's building was simpler, and its unembellished lines were more modern. Managed by Chinese business-people—and less a playhouse for wealthy Europeans than the Cathay—the Park reflected the efficiency, functionality, and entrepreneurialism infusing Shanghai.

Within a few years of the Park's opening, however, Shanghai's golden age came to a grim close. After years of intensifying hostilities with Japan, violent clashes erupted into all-out war in 1937. *Time* magazine described a city under siege in 1941: "Cabarets, with their white slaves, adventurers, opium-runners and hatchetmen, still operate in Shanghai, but ringed about with Japanese bayonets, spies, terrorized by free-firing gunmen, they have lost their glamour."

Park Hotel
LASZLO HUDEC, 1934
Hudec's studio designed some of Shanghai's best modern architecture of the early and mid-twentieth century, much of it influenced by the German Bauhaus. The Park Hotel, Hudec's largest and most famous building, was inspired by skyscrapers seen during a visit to Manhattan.

On the heels of the brutal Japanese occupation and the deprivations of World War II came civil war as Nationalists and Communists vied for power. The strife culminated in the so-called Communist liberation of 1949. Foreigners entirely relinquished Shanghai, but authorities continued to scorn the city for its bourgeois, West-leaning past. The government also suppressed architecture, among other creative professions, as suspiciously individualistic.

In this postwar era, Shanghai went gray. The vibrancy of Nanjing Road's bustling businesses was extinguished. Once beautiful estates were sacked—their owners carried away for reeducation—and divided into apartments for the worker-citizens. (A few were left intact for high officials.) Drab dormancy enveloped the city for decades. Even after 1979, when Deng Xiaoping introduced his Open Door policy to encourage foreign investment, Communist leaders were too wary of Shanghai's capitalist, decadent history to test the free market there. While special concessions enabled cities like Shenzhen to grow from almost nothing into metropolises, Shanghai languished. Not until 1992—and with Deng's emphatic support—was Shanghai recognized as China's once and future commercial and financial center.

The city's industrial importance, and its citizens' inherent entrepreneurialism, made Shanghai's leadership inevitable. There were already signs of foreign investment, with forward-looking Americans among those willing to bet on Shanghai. Ambitious building campaigns began transforming the city. The first rumblings of the construction of a new Shanghai were heard on West Nanjing Road, the

Park Hotel
Renovated to the tastes of the twenty-first century, the Park Hotel's interior now has lavish finishes that would have been considered retro when the hotel opened in the streamlined 1930s. Notwithstanding the cosmetic changes, the structure reveals Hudec's complex sense of space and his intention to dazzle.

result of a concerted effort by the American architect-developer John Portman. Portman's association with China began in 1978, when Deng Xiaoping visited Georgia, home state of then President Jimmy Carter. The Chinese leader was impressed by Portman's Peachtree Center in Atlanta, a hotel-office-mall complex with Portman's signature features, a lofty hotel atrium and exposed glass elevators. To anyone accustomed to the sprawling, concrete-block architecture of Red China, it was otherworldly.

Deng later invited the architect to China as part of an early American business delegation. Thus encouraged, the Portman group established an office in Hong Kong, aiming to build American-style multiuse projects in Chinese cities. But plans for several promising hotel-anchored developments evaporated when a series of people charged with shepherding the contracts through the state bureaucracies disappeared for unknown, perhaps political reasons.

Despite the frustrations, Portman's son Jack continued to pursue business on the mainland, where he was offered numerous sites on the undeveloped outskirts. Jack Portman rejected them all as unsuitable, as the company's experience—and success—had been in or close to existing city centers, such as in Atlanta and Detroit. A turning point came in 1984, when an arrangement was made for land on West Nanjing Road.

On this relatively narrow lot Portman devised a scheme for the Shanghai Centre, which would encompass a seven-hundred-room hotel, 600,000 square feet of residential apartments, and ground-floor shops and restaurants. A huge departure from anything then in China, it attracted investors to the tune of two hundred million dollars. The American Insurance Group became the lead partner; Kajima Corporation, a Japanese construction firm, took a major position; and a multinational syndicate of nineteen financial institutions provided a mortgage. The risks were significant, as Jack Portman noted in an interview while construction was under way. "In China the profit potential is enormous. If you hit a home run, it's going to go way out of the park. But a strikeout is deadly. . . . You can say we're going to make a bloody fortune over there. But in reality, we can be kicked out tomorrow."

Other problems were inherent to building forty-eight stories atop some of the soggiest earth under any major city. Alluvial soil plus seismic building codes called for a massive concrete structure—a marked contrast to the light, glassy atrium towers that had made the Portman name famous in America. The firm's design goal always had been "to open everything up . . . , explode the buildings from the inside, create interior lungs, exterior spaces, and to create a human environment," as John Portman explained. In Shanghai, the solution was to create outdoor spaces by letting light in between concrete construction elements that were frankly Brutalist in style.

Shanghai Centre
JOHN PORTMAN & ASSOCIATES, 1990
Shanghai Centre was one of the first buildings in the new Shanghai to be designed by a Western architect. Its heavy, reinforced-concrete construction, the product of old seismic codes, sharply contrasts with the soaring, airy atrium buildings with which Portman made his name. The central tower houses a hotel with seven hundred rooms; the two flanking towers contain apartments.

Still, the most daunting challenge to this early experiment in direct foreign investment was political. The building was nearly complete when, in 1989, a series of demonstrations for intellectual and democratic freedoms triggered a crackdown by the alarmed government, which sparked Beijing's Tiananmen Square massacre. In the ensuing crisis, Portman's project screeched to a halt. Although work resumed six months later, instability and international condemnation of China's leaders gave rise to other problems, including the hotel operator's withdrawal from Shanghai Centre. A replacement was found, but the disruptions cost the project a decade of financial turmoil.

Nevertheless, Shanghai Centre almost instantly became the city's business and social hub—*the* place to stay for investors, architects, politicians, and others. Though it soon became fashionable to criticize its loud, colorful, postmodern decor—which was going out of style even as it was being built—the center was instrumental in bringing a taste of the contemporary West to Shanghai. Its tenants included a Hard Rock Cafe. A theater in the complex opened with *Sweeney Todd*. In time it even housed one of Shanghai's first Starbucks, where a stream of suited businessmen wait for lattes and young slackers sit with heads bowed over laptops.

Shanghai Centre
The building's seven-story pedestal includes exhibition space, meeting rooms, a thousand-seat theater, and courtyardlike spaces lined by stores and restaurants. The multiple uses make "the Portman," as it's called, the center of activity on West Nanjing Road.

Hotel lobby, Shanghai Centre
The interior of the hotel in the central tower was meant to dazzle a design-starved Shanghai.

Tomorrow Square
JOHN PORTMAN & ASSOCIATES, 2003
This futuristic sixty-story tower
contains a six-level retail atrium,
thirty-six floors of executive
apartments, and a J. W. Marriott
Hotel. The exterior design was meant
to reflect the multiple uses within.
For example, the building's forty-
five-degree rotation at the thirty-
seventh floor indicates where the
hotel begins. The architects described
the pierced peak as a symbol of
Shanghai's upward reach: incomplete
and with infinite possibility.

Tomorrow Square
The building's distinct geometric shifts presaged the torqued and twisting skyscrapers now seen in advanced high-rises worldwide.

J. W. Marriott Hotel, Tomorrow Square
JOHN PORTMAN & ASSOCIATES, 2003
The street-level elevator lobby (right) echoes the monumentality of the building's exterior. The hotel, beginning on the thirty-seventh floor, is designed to take advantage of the expansive views, with quietly decorated rooms wrapped in wide glass windows. The bathroom (above right) is outfitted in Art Deco style, recalling Shanghai's golden age.

Plaza 66

KOHN PEDERSEN FOX, 2002

Plaza 66 is the tallest building in a neighborhood of tall buildings, but what distinguished it was the lightness of its steel and glass exterior. In the mid-1990s, when it was designed, building codes were being rewritten as construction technology improved. New confidence in modern architecture's stable foundations encouraged architects to make their towers soar. Architect Jamie von Klemperer called further attention to Plaza 66 by topping it with a finial suggesting a wick or flame.

Shanghai Centre also attracted other new development to West Nanjing Road, which became Puxi's focal point. By 1993 the fallout from Tiananmen had dissipated, and the pent-up impulse to invest in China was stronger than ever. A long-term land lease just east of Portman's Shanghai Centre went for a reported three hundred million dollars, a princely sum at the time. The investor was Hong Kong financier Ronnie Chan, who recognized that his location in the once vibrant, now tattered neighborhood represented Shanghai's "hundred percent corner"—in retail parlance, the place with the highest traffic, highest sales, and therefore highest rents. He wanted to maximize the site's commercial potential with a "spirited design," said his architect, Jamie von Klemperer of the New York firm Kohn Pedersen Fox.

What Von Klemperer came up with was Plaza 66, Puxi's tallest building, comprising two office towers with a shopping mall at the base. Despite Plaza 66's assertively modern aspect, the architect claims to have been influenced by the old *lilongs* across the street. *Lilongs* (loosely translated as "homes in alleys") are the tightly spaced, two- or three-story row houses that were once ubiquitous in Puxi. Collectively, they made up dense, low-rise neighborhoods, typically enclosed by plain plaster walls with randomly placed gates.

Inspired by what he called "a patchwork of housing . . . an intricate network of alleyways," Von Klemperer's design for Plaza 66 echoed some of the *lilong* block's features. At street level, its masonry walls are punctuated irregularly by sections of glass, and the scale of the multiple entrances to the five-story mall was meant to be reminiscent of *lilong* gates. The architect hoped that the subtle familiarity would induce passersby to enter freely, as they might enter an old neighborhood, move easily through, and later exit from a different door.

The mall and first tower were completed in 2002, and Plaza 66 was as successful as Chan had predicted. Its architecture is hardly restrained, but Von Klemperer defended its brashness as a valid approach when Shanghai swung open its doors to the outside world. "My reaction to the wildness of Shanghai architecture early on was that it seemed tawdry," he said. "But what I came to see in the skyscrapers was a kind of vernacular that justifies itself."

Despite the city's rapid and radical development, change has not been complete. Though most of old Shanghai has been unceremoniously bulldozed to make way for the future, the surge of new construction has been accompanied by a belated appreciation of historic architecture—and an eleventh-hour attempt to salvage it. Shanghai's interest in preservation has focused on the few remaining *lilong* neighborhoods. Many of the houses there were designed and built carefully, sometimes luxuriously, but about ninety percent of Shanghai's *lilongs* are said to have been razed before the municipal government recognized their value.

Shanghai Exhibition Center

ANDERLEV AND JISLOVA, 1956

Built as the Sino-Soviet Friendship Mansion, the center displays the massivity and ornate neoclassicism common in Communist bloc buildings. Its juxtaposition with Plaza 66's modern tower—which has a shopping mall on its lower levels and business offices above—demonstrates Shanghai's dizzying transition in recent years.

Plaza 66
Even before the construction of the upscale shopping mall at the base of Plaza 66, the stretch of West Nanjing Road it sits on was known by real estate developers as Shanghai's hundred percent retail corner, the geographic center of the city's growing consumerism.

Shanghai's traditional *lilong* neighborhoods, mazes of lanes and row houses, inspired some elements of Plaza 66, where narrow passages and terraces add interest and complexity.

The first large-scale redevelopment of a *lilong* neighborhood began almost by chance in the late 1990s. Officials of Shanghai's Luwan district, in the old French Concession, sought—atypically—to build on a smaller, more human scale than the towers that were suddenly scraping Shanghai's sky. They planned to develop the neighborhood around the Communist Party Museum, a former schoolhouse where Mao Zedong, Chou En-lai, and others founded the Chinese Communist party in 1921.

The project went to Vincent Lo of Shui On Development, a real estate tycoon from Hong Kong. Lo brought in planners who proposed devoting the area to retail and replacing most of the existing structures. At the last minute Lo had second thoughts and sought a new approach. He found Ben Wood, a Boston-based architect who had worked on many historic restorations, including Boston's Faneuil Hall. Wood was the only architect to tell Lo that the *lilong* houses could be saved. He was dazzled by their architectural authenticity. "What you've got here is the equivalent of Siena in China," he told Lo. It happened that Lo had just returned from a vacation in Italy and understood the analogy immediately. Wood got the job.

Condemned *lilong* buildings
As Shanghai modernized toward the end of the twentieth century, *lilongs* were razed without a second thought. About ninety percent of them were destroyed before preservationists and designers discovered ways to adapt the row houses to new uses. Once ubiquitous, they are now scarce and considered precious.

***Lilong* lane**
Lilong neighborhoods, filled with row houses along narrow lanes, were built all over Shanghai beginning in the late 1880s to accommodate the large number of people migrating to the city, many of them escaping political turmoil and other dangers.

He did not entirely or worshipfully preserve what was there; rather, he adapted the space for contemporary needs. One whole row of houses was taken out to widen a main thoroughfare, and large windows were cut into the sides of many brick walls, providing new boutiques with natural light and display space. A glass cube was fit between two buildings to house a hair salon; a large house was vacated and restored as a conference center.

Xintiandi reconceived the possibilities of the *lilong* neighborhood and much else, including the way Shanghainese dined out. The city's traditional restaurants were large and formal, with big groups seated at round tables in the front and live poultry housed and slaughtered in the back. To Wood, big restaurants made no sense in Xintiandi's modestly scaled neighborhood.

Serendipitously, he met the owner of a small bistro elsewhere in the French Concession. The owner, a Taiwanese, said modern restaurateurs from all over Asia were looking for Shanghai locations; some of their eateries ultimately filled Xintiandi. Many offered al fresco dining, previously unknown in China and soon widely popular. None of the restaurants in Xintiandi needed space for live poultry. Shanghai's new entertainment rialto became such a success that "to Xintiandi" is now a verb, meaning to transform an old neighborhood with fancy renovations and windfall rents.

Xintiandi
WOOD + ZAPATA, 2002
The Xintiandi entertainment district was carved from an old *lilong* neighborhood, and its success marked a turning point in Shanghai's preservation movement.

Beside a man-made lake and amid a profoundly altered landscape, patches of the old urban fabric survive.

Xintiandi
Although Xintiandi did not retain all the original elements—for example, a whole row of houses was razed to widen the main thoroughfare through the shopping district, pictured here—it did highlight the possibilities of historical preservation. Adapting the old brick *lilong* buildings to contemporary use, Xintiandi's architect cut large windows into the walls, flooding the interiors with natural light. He also fit a glass cube between two buildings, expanding the space for a hair salon.

Xintiandi

The *lilongs* of old Shanghai were designed with extreme economy of space. Their evocative, narrow lanes provided the architects designing the Xintiandi entertainment district with variety, mystery, and inspiration.

Xintiandi's chic, intimate eateries sharply contrasted with the brightly lit halls and banquet tables that previously had defined dining out in Shanghai.

Another important work of preservation unfolded in a sprawling industrial zone on the banks of Suzhou Creek, now described as Shanghai's Soho. Even as some of the factories and warehouses there were being razed to make way for high-rises, others were being developed as lofts and colonized by artists, galleries, design shops, and restaurants.

Shanghai's loft movement began when Taiwanese architect and interior designer Deng Kunyan surveyed a stretch of the creek, at the time one of the world's most polluted bodies of water, and found at least thirty buildings that could be redeveloped. He purchased his first, now called Suzhou Creek Warehouse, in 1998. It had both historical cachet as the former warehouse of one of Shanghai's most notorious gangsters and, more important, flowing, open interiors. Deng put up glass walls and located his studio and a party space there. Shanghai's arts community noticed the charms of the place and followed.

As the area became chic, real estate speculators' interest intensified, and tensions grew between the monied developers and the creative loft dwellers. In 2002 several highly regarded galleries were evicted from one well-loved loft building, which was soon razed and replaced by condominiums. That demolition marked a turning point, as government officials stepped in, designated several miles of creekside buildings historic landmarks, and announced that they intended to enforce preservation regulations.

Suzhou Creek conversions
The former textile mill at 50 Moganshan Road (above and left) had few of the charms of older factories and warehouses along Suzhou Creek, but its size and availability made it a center for Shanghai's art galleries and design studios. One tenant, architect Chen Xudong, undertook the renovation, completed in 2004. Chen's firm, DAtrans, modernized the brick structures in part by adapting the original steel-frame windows, providing abundant light.

Price Waterhouse Coopers Centre
PALMER AND TURNER, 2003
The Price Waterhouse building (opposite) hovers over the *lilong* house where Mao Zedong, Chou En-lai, and others founded the Chinese Communist party in 1921; that building is now the Communist Party Museum. Ironically, the museum's impending celebration of the fiftieth anniversary of the People's Republic, in 1999, was the impetus for salvaging the *lilong* neighborhood that became Xintiandi, a glittering capitalist showcase whose success inspired commercial construction nearby.

With so much of old Shanghai knocked down and appreciation of the remaining vintage structures growing, prices for historic houses in Puxi skyrocketed. By 2007 a desirable old row house could fetch a million dollars or more. Investments of that magnitude tend to inspire extensive restorations. As one architect specializing in such work found, digging into a property's original character can be like archaeology, yielding insights about eras long past while also inspiring up-to-date designs.

When Spencer Dodington undertook the refurbishment of one *lilong* house, he researched other surviving houses in the neighborhood, discovered old layouts, and had original details replicated. As work progressed, Dodington was surprised to find a walled-over door that connected the house to one next door. A little more investigation revealed that a row of six houses had once been connected to one another. With some persistence Dodington found an old neighbor who remembered that a wealthy cotton trader had owned the houses—one for each of his six wives. (Vestiges of polygamy still lingered from the days of imperial China.) But the cotton trader left the mainland for Taiwan in 1949, rightly suspecting that the Communists who had come to power would both frown on his domestic arrangements and end his career as a market maker.

The connecting doors inspired by the trader's multiple marriages are not just an evocative memento of life in old Shanghai; they are a haunting reminder that, after a half century of wrenching change, Shanghai society has come almost full circle. While polygamy has been firmly consigned to the past, capitalism is resoundingly back in favor. And the old *lilongs* abandoned by those fleeing Communism are now the gleamingly refurbished homes of a new generation of affluent Shanghainese.

Art Deco House,
French Concession, 1930s
Western architects flocked to
Shanghai in the 1920s and 1930s,
when the Great Depression
suppressed building almost
everywhere else in the world.
They brought with them the
Art Deco trend that then prevailed
in Europe and the United States.
The Shanghainese version of the
style tended to be stripped down
to essentials.

**Private residence,
French Concession, c. 1930**
In 2005 American designer Spencer
Dodington, a Shanghai resident,
refurbished this row house in one
of the few *lilong* neighborhoods
to escape demolition. He created a
fashionable residence, with Bauhaus-
style doors and windows and a
spareness that is modern in character
but also consonant with Chinese
design.

Dodington residence
INTERIOR BY SPENCER DODINGTON, 2005
In his own home in the former
French Concession, Dodington
assembled a modern apartment
from pieces evoking Shanghai's past.
He found some of them in antiques
shops and had others re-created
by craftsmen. The curtains were
inspired, he said, by something he
saw in a period American movie.

THE SUBURBS Around the World and Back

Longyang Road Station

EAST CHINA ARCHITECTURE
DESIGN STUDIO, 2002

The station's simple design is a rare success for Shanghai's maglev transit system. The underused high-speed train line can be seen as an expensive error of urban planning.

WITH MUCH FANFARE, and with China's president and Germany's chancellor cutting the ribbon, Shanghai's maglev transportation line debuted in 2002. One of the fastest trains in the world, the German-built, $1.2 billion maglev represented the first commercial use of magnetic levitation technology. The sleek, bulletlike trains levitate magnetically above a monorail—eliminating the friction of steel wheel on steel track—and course along at two hundred miles an hour. During the ceremonial first trip Premier Zhu Rongji hailed it as "a miracle."

The track slices through the countryside for nineteen miles between Pudong International Airport and a terminus at Longyang Road Station. The station, a large tube sheathed in steel louvers, is a structure of admirable restraint. Simple, partly enclosed, and partly open to the sky, it eschews the futuristic eccentricity for which Pudong is known. It is the work of ECADI, Shanghai's immense design institute. "We wanted something modern," said one of the station's lead designers. "That was the most important thing."

Despite its architectural success, Longyang Road Station seems destined to be little discussed and largely uninfluential in the development of Shanghai's public buildings. The station's quiet modernism is nearly lost amid the cacophony of Pudong's postmodernist construction. And even excellent design cannot overcome a badly chosen location. The Longyang terminus at the edge of Pudong is hard to reach, and the line is largely unused as an airport link. Thus far, the maglev is a billion-dollar train to nowhere, a commercial failure.

A decade into Shanghai's building boom, the maglev's poor results provided another harsh lesson in the necessity of urban planning. In fact, even as miscalculations were dooming the maglev, change was in the works. In 2001 then Mayor Chen Liangyu and other officials unveiled a plan to shift Shanghai's growth from the city center to its outskirts. They were spurred by the city's obvious disorder, by reports that the earth beneath Pudong was sinking by as much as a half inch per year, and by predictions of unflagging population growth. Projections were that the already overcrowded city would continue to swell by thirty percent, reaching 23.4 million by 2020. The development of housing was critical, as workers continued to migrate to the city from the countryside and the construction of new office towers displaced neighborhoods of Shanghai residents.

The official plan to promote the suburbs, called One City/Nine Towns, sited major satellite towns as far as thirty miles away; they were to accommodate a million residents quickly, with additional housing later. The plan was audacious in scale but controversial in its details, including the idea of creating each town in the architectural style of a different nation: Germany, Italy, Sweden, England, and even old China, among others. While officials may have thought the plan invoked Shanghai's roots in disparate cultures, others feared the result would be theme park–style villages largely divorced from local context. But, as was customary in China, the naysayers went unheard and a top-down, unilateral decision put the One City/Nine Towns plan into effect. Not even Chen's disgrace in a 2006 corruption scandal and his subsequent jail sentence sidetracked the project.

The city's deputy director of planning, Wu Jiang, a former professor who was spearheading Shanghai's preservation efforts at the time, was unenthusiastic about the plan's foreign themes. He preferred to see something Chinese developed. The reliance on European imagery seemed likely to resurrect memories of Shanghai's past humiliations as a de facto colony—and to surrender Shanghai's next phase of development, like the previous ones, to architects without roots in China. Some Western architects likewise questioned the decision.

"At first I asked, what is this festival of the world all about?" said Augusto Cagnardi, a principal of Gregotti Associati, the Milan-based firm that came to be largely responsible for designing Pujiang, the town meant to have an Italian accent. Ultimately he concluded, "The historic parts of Shanghai have always been created by other cultures and not the Chinese."

In fact, financially able home buyers in twenty-first-century China seemed eager to embrace Western-style housing in the new suburbs, all of which catered to the newly wealthy. "The truth is that most Chinese would like to go abroad, and this gives them the dream," said Wu. Whatever his concerns about the plan's details, Wu approved of its broad strokes. "Actually, a city shouldn't be too, too big," he said. "So the only conclusion is that we should organize several new cities around Shanghai instead of one central city."

As it went forward, the One City/Nine Towns plan proved to be a turning point for Shanghai. For the first time in the city's history, a master plan was conceived, implemented, and essentially followed. Results varied widely from town to town, partly because plans were overseen and executed by a different set of district officials in each, partly because of shifting economic forces and the various aesthetic ambitions of the architects involved. Yet some towns exhibited real architectural progress and demonstrated that orderly growth was possible.

The evolution of Cagnardi's Pujiang New Town, south of Pudong and east of the Huangpu River, serves as a good case study. The first phase, five thousand

Luxury villas, Pujiang
GREGOTTI ASSOCIATI, 2005
When plans for new suburbs, each in the style of a different country, were announced, some feared Shanghai would be encircled by Disneyesque replicas of medieval towns. Instead, most of the architects involved brought a modern sensibility to the project, as seen in Gregotti's contemporary designs for the Italian-themed town.

homes and a town center, began with the obligatory competition. That Gregotti Associati won this round was not surprising. The firm had done similar work in Europe and had *guanxi*, or connections, with Shanghai officials, having consulted on the restoration of the Bund. And, after all, Pujiang was to be the "Italian" suburb, and the architects were from Milan.

The master plan suggested that Pujiang officials sought a version of old Italy, with avenues, piazzas, and canals. Cagnardi himself had imagined a mosaiclike development, with "a small piece of Venice, a small piece of Rome" cobbled together. But when it came to developing the details, the architects were surprised by the client's intentions. The real estate people in charge of the project had done test marketing and found that middle- and upper-middle-class buyers were attracted to modern Italian design, not the Renaissance. So instead of a faux Firenze, Cagnardi said, "We would design a town much as we would do it normally." Thus the town displayed the spare, even stark lines of industrial-age modernism, with large courtyards and dramatic interiors.

If anything, Pujiang was more elaborate than an equivalent Gregotti project would have been in Italy. An example was the town's sales-promotion center, meant to romance people into buying homes that initially averaged $250,000. The sales center was to be converted to a cultural center when the first phase of Pujiang New Town was completed and sold, and nothing, it seemed, was

Low-rise apartments, Pujiang
GREGOTTI ASSOCIATI, 2005
Shanghai's cities, like ancient Roman towns, were traditionally laid out in a rectangular grid, with the regularity broken by diagonals. Pujiang New Town drew upon such plans, with open spaces providing a human scale. They could be described as piazzas, in deference to the suburb's Italian theme, but are actually semiprivate yards.

High-rise apartments, Pujiang
GREGOTTI ASSOCIATI, 2005
Pujiang New Town will eventually cover about six square miles and house eighty thousand people, mostly commuters to Shanghai and their families. Home prices started just below $100,000, beyond the reach of most Chinese, whose average household income is less than $7,000.

Sales Promotion Center, Pujiang
GREGOTTI ASSOCIATI, 2004
Pujiang's sales center (below), which will convert to a cultural center when the town is fully occupied, suggests the influence of twentieth-century modernism, yet the intimate open spaces scattered throughout the building are reminiscent of Chinese gardens.

too good or too costly for this building. "What we designed was all marble," explained Cagnardi. "It was something we would never have dared to propose in Italy. But here they took one look at it and said, 'go ahead.'"

Still, there were challenges, including the tricky navigation between European design and Chinese execution. "They gave us only a month to design this building, which we did," Cagnardi said. "And when we gave them the plans, they asked, 'Why so much detail?'" The Chinese were accustomed to making working drawings themselves from foreign-designed schemes—a process, Cagnardi realized, that could damage his firm's careful design beyond recognition. The Gregotti team worked closely with its Chinese counterparts on what Cagnardi called "a process of reeducation," and the Chinese architects showed a sharp willingness to learn. The collaboration—considerably more fruitful than that of larger-scale projects just a few years before in Shanghai—demonstrated an encouraging progression along the learning curve for architecture in China. In fact, one of the unanticipated benefits of the Nine Towns plan was the in-depth education it provided the many native architects who were, by law, involved in every project.

As had happened in Pujiang, some of the other suburbs adopted an unexpectedly modern aspect as they took shape. In Anting New Town, in the Jiading district northwest of Shanghai, a Germanic theme was an almost logical extension of the fact that Volkswagen had long operated an auto factory there. Despite concerns that Anting would be filled with rathskellers and glockenspiels, the final result was no more an evocation of old Bavaria than Pujiang was of Renaissance Italy. But the difference in Anting was that the clients had dreamed of developing a Rhineland village in the Yangtze River Delta. It fell to the architects, Frankfurt's Albert Speer & Partner (AS&P), to persuade the decision makers of the virtues of a more modern approach.

The firm, owned by the son of Nazi architect Albert Speer, had won the competition for Anting on the basis of its master plan, a generally circular footprint with a "hierarchy of urban spaces." Jiading officials saw something medieval in this broad outline and envisioned "a traditional . . . European small city design," as AS&P's Johannes Dell dismissively called it. That was exactly what the firm did not want to do.

"If you promise the people to have a modern standard in their houses, and if the buildings themselves look like they are five hundred years old, what you have is something like a Disneyland," said Dell. "It is a fake." To convince the Chinese that such an approach would be a poor strategy for city development, AS&P took its clients to Weimar, Germany, to see Bauhaus architecture in its birthplace. "It took a lot of preaching," said Dell. In the end, the clients understood that "the marketing would be very much easier with something more modern than with this completely retrospective design."

Apartments, Anting
ALBERT SPEER & PARTNER, 2005
Architects at AS&P vetoed any suggestion of filling Shanghai's German-themed suburb with half-timber houses and glockenspiels. They instead sold the clients on a Bauhaus-inspired modern style with an emphatic sense of form and color.

Shanghai International Circuit, Anting
TILKE INGENIEURE UND ARCHITEKTEN, 2004
Expanding on its history of automotive manufacturing, Anting opened a Formula One racetrack in 2004, securing its position as Shanghai's motor city. At $300 million, it was the world's most expensive Formula One track when completed. Plans are to develop an automobile theme park on the site. Hermann Tilke, a leading architect of Formula One circuits, laid out the 3.4-mile track's fourteen turns with driver safety and spectator sight lines in mind. From the air the course resembles the Chinese character *shang* (part of the word *shanghai*), which means "high" or "ascend."

Shanghai International Circuit
Building the Formula One track and grandstands for nearly two hundred thousand spectators on unstable, wet ground required a floating platform under the racing pavement. Above the grandstands, twenty-six "lotus-leaf" canopies shield spectators from the elements.

Shanghai International Circuit
The complex was intended to
establish Anting as a world-class
automotive city, so in addition to
the racetrack it includes business
facilities for the auto industry.
Restaurants, a hotel, and exhibition
space line the lakes and lagoons
coursing through the site.

Enhance Anting Golf Club
GOETTSCH PARTNERS, 2006
Golf has a corporate image in China, and the most lavish clubs, like this one, are ultramodern. The Anting complex includes an eighteen-hole golf course and clubhouse, a business hotel, apartments, a spa, restaurants, and meeting rooms.

The imposing entry to the low-rise golf clubhouse, with heavily rusticated granite and monolithic stairways, gives way to a twenty-six-foot-high atrium (overleaf). The glass, natural light, and false ceiling with upturned panels are suggestive of the weightless heavens.

But not all of the Nine Towns avoided the look of what Dell called "a Disneyland." In Songjiang, the suburb slated as English, the Thames Town neighborhood verges on being a historic re-creation. Georgian and Tudor facades rise above cobbled streets in the village center, which also boasts a fish-and-chips shop and a number of bright red telephone booths. The scenography continues outward from the village along winding streets, where miniature manor houses—initially priced at five hundred thousand dollars and up—sit upon broad lawns.

Thames Town's embrace of all things British—however curious, given the historic tensions between China and England—is part of the architectural expression of plans for Songjiang to become China's Oxbridge. It will be home to eight universities, some of which are already under construction. But there's more than a touch of escapist fantasy in the affluent suburb's unbridled Anglophilia. At one of the first ceremonies in Thames Town's Gothic chapel (unconsecrated and used as a reception hall), a kilt-wearing groom married a bride adorned with a tartan sash.

Even so, Songjiang's gated enclaves are not exclusively British in design. Another neighborhood, Santa Barbara Villa, was created in the very image of Southern California. It is the handiwork of Bruce Halferty, a Los Angeles architect with a design studio in Shanghai, who in 2001 was invited to compete for the development, not far from Thames Town. As Halferty explained, another designer

Thames Town
W. S. ATKINS, 2004
Thames Town, the English-style neighborhood in Shanghai's Songjiang district, promises to be one of Shanghai's more exclusive suburbs, with prices averaging $500,000 for a miniature manor. While the contemporary taste for traditional English designs may seem incongruous, Shanghai's architectural history is filled with similar examples.

had already been chosen in the back rooms, but a competition was mandated by law. He was able to overturn the predetermined outcome with designs in the Santa Barbara Mission style, offering both a voguish foreignness and an inherent simplicity that allowed for varied configurations from a few basic templates. The developers would be able to build for low prices and sell high.

Plans for the new suburb of Qingpu were radically different from the other Nine Towns. Instead of importing a theme from abroad, Qingpu was based on the look and feel of old China. That kind of contextualism was rare in Shanghai, but Qingpu, a large district in the Yangtze Delta north of the city, was a fitting site for such an experiment. Covered with marshes and wetlands, laced by canals, and dotted by so-called water towns, some of which date back hundreds of years, Qingpu offered a distinctive landscape and a rich history to draw upon. The new buildings, inspired by the architecture of the old towns and designed to be in harmony with the terrain, are quieter and less obtrusive than the usual new development in and around Shanghai.

Zhouzhuang Water Town
The ancient water towns of the Yangtze Delta north of Shanghai provide a sense of history and tranquility almost totally absent in the city just an hour away. Zhouzhuang is a pristine example, still almost untouched. Zhujiajiao, another old water town some miles closer to Shanghai, also retains an authentic character, although development has brought change.

In fact, Qingpu is the most promising of the Nine Towns, largely because its design addresses local conditions, but also because experience has sifted out many bad ideas. While influenced by the past, the architecture does not replicate it. Rather, the area's history infuses truly modern work.

A central figure in modern architecture's evolution in Qingpu is Dr. Sun Jiwei, who was made vice district chief in 2002. A trained architect and a former professor at Tongji University, Sun recognized that good design was also good business. His sensibility derived in part from his experience overseeing the construction of Xintiandi, where historic preservation led to great commercial success.

Sun had two large American planning firms, Sasaki Associates and SWA Group, study Qingpu and its prospects for development. SWA first identified the delta region's rich water features and historical elements, such as Zhujiajiao, a charming and largely intact water town. Robert Jacob, SWA's principal in charge of the project, explained that only after understanding what Qingpu had to preserve should the district planners superimpose roads and public infrastructure.

Jacob remembered how the authorities marveled at that approach to planning—an inversion of the usual Chinese way, which began with roads and housing and only later considered conservation. Jacob believed their receptiveness stemmed at least partly from the first presentation being held not in government offices but in SWA's Shanghai studio, where officials felt free to ask questions and to probe the limitations of their typical process.

In the end, the two American firms' master plans fared as most do: They were introduced in political councils with gravitas, regarded with interest by relevant officials, and then relegated to a filing cabinet. Yet SWA's environmental themes had a perceptible influence on subsequent efforts to develop the area, which highlighted Qingpu's historic and natural assets even as construction of homes for tens of thousands of residents got under way.

As Qingpu's most intact historical element, Zhujiajiao inspired the design of the district at large. Zhujiajiao had been an active trading center for centuries and was known as the Venice of China. With its picturesque lanes, gardens, water-

ways, and stone bridges, it was a longtime tourist destination. To build on that strength, Sun brought in one of China's most important native-born architects, Chang Yung Ho, a Berkeley-trained modernist. His charge was to create a new cluster of restaurants, shops, and a hotel that blended with Zhujiajiao's tight urban fabric. Using steel and glass, Chang created narrow lanes and low elevations that corresponded with those of the existing town. His varied palette of wood, clay tile, and frosted glass (suggesting traditional rice-paper windows) introduced a "time element," as Chang described it, the illusion that the individual structures were built at different points in the past. Chang's section of Zhujiajiao, begun in 2006, has an authentic feel, not at all like a stage set. The spare design echoes the old town's simplicity and functionality.

Cambridge Water Town, a new neighborhood that began taking shape on the edge of Zhujiajiao in 2003, is also inspired by the old town, with a decidedly modern result. Here in the Yangtze Delta, architect Ben Wood proved—as he had in Shanghai's *lilong* neighborhoods—that the new can coexist with the old, to the benefit of both. At neither Xintiandi nor Cambridge is his work a profound exercise in historicism. However, Wood's modern designs for Cambridge suggest a contemporary evocation of the district's ancient water towns, with a similar scale and an essential conservatism. The footbridges and canals have clear Ming dynasty antecedents, yet the sleek town houses offer the conveniences and luxury that financially able Chinese seek. "It's a sort of transformation of the vernacular water town urban typology with clean modern lines," said Wood.

Zhouzhuang Water Town
With narrow canals lined by well-preserved homes and spanned by stone footbridges, China's water towns suggest Venice's Asian counterparts.

Cambridge Water Town
BEN WOOD STUDIO SHANGHAI, 2005–6
Cambridge Water Town's public buildings, such as the sales center (opposite, at top and bottom left), as well as its private houses (bottom right) emulate the scale and layout of Zhouzhuang, Zhujiajiao, and the Yangtze Delta's other ancient canal towns.

Sales center, Cambridge Water Town
Sleekly modern buildings like the
sales center (opposite), which
eventually will be converted to
a community center, mimic the
openness of the traditional buildings
that lined the old water town canals.

Villa, Cambridge Water Town
BEN WOOD STUDIO SHANGHAI, 2005–6
When completed, Cambridge Water
Town will offer more than eight
hundred residences, ranging in size
from 1,400 to 3,230 square feet.
With screenlike walls, prominent
eaves, and lacquered finishes,
their modernism echoes Chinese
design traditions.

An exceptionally sophisticated and innovative example of how Qingpu's new architecture aims to blend with its surroundings is Chang Yung Ho's proposal for Heron Lake, a housing development on several hundred acres around a wetland. The plan, by a Chinese developer known for more conventional projects, includes environmentally sensitive features like low-tech gabions for flood control and the planting of hundreds of native trees, such as camphor, gingko, and willow.

The houses are meant to subtly complement the landscape. Chang designed minimalist, glassy pavilions with passive solar elements, terraced gardens, and indoor-outdoor spaces with eaves reminiscent of Frank Lloyd Wright's (which themselves recall Asian antecedents). For the clubhouse, Chang designed a series of curvilinear structures extending over several small islands and connected by walkways and bridges. If approved, Heron Lake could be one of the most splendid developments in all of Qingpu.

What makes such a project possible is the monied client's interest in living in harmony with nature. What could make it difficult is growing political resistance to the tastes of monied clients, as well as a recent discouragement of high-end developments in favor of middle-income housing. The question remains whether district officials will see the Heron Lake proposal as state-of-the-art architecture or as an all too exclusive enclave for the rich.

But even on the drawing board, Heron Lake is clear evidence of the maturation of China's architectural talent. Chang is among the most eminent of a new generation of architects that is pushing modernism's boundaries in China and beyond. Another is Ma Qingyun, who, like Chang, not only practices in China but serves as dean of a major American architecture school. (Chang is at the Massachusetts Institute of Technology, and Ma is at the University of Southern California.)

Ma was trained in America and worked for Kohn Pedersen Fox in New York for several years before establishing a practice in Shanghai. One of his most distinctive projects in China is Thumb Island, a government and community center in the new, most densely populated part of Qingpu.

Ma came to the commission after several competitions had failed to produce an acceptable design. As Ma described it, officials were demanding a seeming contradiction: a monumental building that highlighted a small lake on the edge of the site. Ma skillfully incorporated the project's disparate elements into a simple, yet unprecedented, curving form, using the prestressed concrete technology commonly used for highway overpasses. The result is powerfully modern, but the center blends almost seamlessly with the natural environment. The building overlaps the shore and rises in the shape of a mound, like an earthwork. Its rounded surface is a veritable parkland, lined with walking paths, planted with grass and garden plots, and dotted with benches.

Thumb Island
MA QINGYUN, 2007
Ma's contradictory objectives for the government and community center were to create a monumental structure and to highlight the relatively small adjacent lake. His solution was a building engineered somewhat like a highway overpass, which proved not just harmonious with the landscape but virtually part of it.

Thumb Island
The center's curving forms are covered with plantings, even on the rooftops, blending the building with its setting and making it into a public park.

Thumb Island
Though Qingpu New Town is not historic in the manner of Zhujiajiao and other nearby water towns, it too is inspired by local history and conditions. The nature and scale of local waterways provided a leitmotif for new development such as the Thumb Island center.

As Qingpu's best buildings demonstrate, Shanghai's architecture finally is coming into its own after years of colonial influence, a long architectural drought enforced by the Cultural Revolution, and a period when most new buildings were simply the gaudy manifestations of exuberant new wealth. Significantly, some of the greatest advancements are being ushered in by Chinese architects. Their work foreshadows for China a powerful contemporary architecture that negotiates "the delicate combination [of] the global and the local," as Chang Yung Ho put it in a 2005 interview with *BusinessWeek*.

Another encouraging sign is the focus on urban planning that characterized the development of One City/Nine Towns. Perhaps Shanghai is learning from the past and preparing to bury its mistakes as it hurtles into the future. Ma Qingyun suggested as much himself.

In a 2004 interview with a French magazine, Ma recounted a conversation with planning officials about the city's need for green space. His tongue-in-cheek proposal was to identify a beltway of skyscrapers with obsolete designs and climbing vacancy rates, abandon them, and let trees and vegetation "sort of erode into them." Serious or not, Ma's scheme for an architectural graveyard underscores how Shanghai's architecture is evolving just as swiftly as the city is growing.

BIBLIOGRAPHY

Balfour, Alan, and Zheng Shiling. *World Cities: Shanghai.* Chichester, England, and Hoboken, N.J.: Wiley-Academy Press, 2002.

Beaver, Robyn, ed. *The Architecture of Adrian Smith, SOM: Toward a Sustainable Future.* Victoria, Australia: Images Publishing Group, 2007.

Clément, Pierre. *Arte Charpentier and Partners, Architects.* Dalian, China: Dalian University of Technology Press, 2005.

Datz, Christian, ed. *Shanghai Architecture and Design.* Kempen, Germany: Te Neues Publishing Company, 2005.

Denison, Edward, and Guang Yu Ren. *Building Shanghai: The Story of China's Gateway.* Chichester, England, and Hoboken, N.J.: Wiley-Academy Press, 2006.

Goldberger, Paul. "Shanghai Surprise." *The New Yorker* 81, no. 42 (December 26, 2005): 144.

Hawthorne, Christopher. "Shanghai: Sky's the Limit." *Los Angeles Times*, February 27, 2005.

Hietkamp, Lenore. "The Park Hotel, Shanghai (1931–1934) and Its Architect, Laszlo Hudec (1893–1958): 'Tallest Building in the Far East' as Metaphor for Pre-Communist Shanghai." Master's thesis, University of Victoria, British Columbia, 1998.

Jodidio, Philip. *Paul Andreu, Architect.* Basel, Switzerland: Birkhäuser, 2004.

Johnston, Tess. *A Last Look: Western Architecture in Old Shanghai.* Hong Kong: Old China Hand Press, 1993.

Kingwell, Mark. "The City of Tomorrow: Searching for the Future of Architecture in Shanghai." *Harper's Magazine* 310, no. 1857 (February 2005): 62–71.

Olds, Chris. "Globalizing Shanghai: The 'Global Intelligence Corps' and the Building of Pudong." In *Emerging World Cities in Pacific Asia*, edited by Lo Fu-Chen. Tokyo: United Nations University Press, 1997.

Pearson, Clifford. "China: Moving Heaven and Earth and Doing It Faster than You Thought Possible." *Architectural Record* 192, no. 3 (March 2004): 71–73.

Pridmore, Jay. "Introduction." In *Goettsch Partners: Selected and Current Works.* Victoria, Australia: Images Publishing Group, 2007.

Rowe, Peter G., and Seng Kuan. *Shanghai: Architecture and Urbanism for Modern China.* Munich: Prestel Publishing, 2004.

"Shanghai." *Fortune*, January 1935.

Shanghai Architecture and Design. Cologne: Daab Publishing, 2005.

Streshinsky, Shirley. "Shanghai Sees the Light." *Preservation Magazine*, September–October 2000.

Wilson, G. L. "Architecture, Interior Decoration and Building in Shanghai Twenty Years Ago and Today." *The China Journal* 12 (May 1930).

Zhao, Chunlan. "From Shikumen to New-Style: A Rereading of Lilong Housing in Modern Shanghai." *The Journal of Architecture* 9, no. 1 (March 2004): 49–76.

ACKNOWLEDGMENTS

This portrait of Shanghai's architecture was researched, written, and illustrated with the help and guidance of many people in China, North America, and Europe. Most are architects, and many have worked to open the door to modern design in China in a period of new (if cautious) freedoms and enthusiasm for the future.

My thanks go to many. In Shanghai they include Ben Wood and Delphine Yip of Studio Shanghai; Ma Qingyun of MADA s.p.a.m. (and Zelda Wong, his assistant at the University of Southern California, where he serves as dean); Henry Wu and Suzanne Lorenz of Haipo Architects; Wu Jiang, deputy director of planning in the Shanghai Municipal Government; and Ling Den Li of East China Architecture and Design Institute. Thanks also to Chang Yung Ho, a dean at the Massachusetts Institute of Technology whose studio is based in Beijing.

In North America: Jim Goettsch, James Zheng, and Matt Larson of Goettsch Partners, Chicago; Sandi Pei of Pei Partners, New York; Tom Rowe and Patrick O'Leary of Michael Graves & Associates, Princeton, N.J.; Walt Jackson, Grace Tam, Emily Munnell, and Jack Portman of John Portman & Associates, Atlanta; Jamie von Klemperer and Kansas Waugh of Kohn Pedersen Fox, New York; Liu Xiaoguang of RTKL, Los Angeles; Adrian Smith, Kim Medici, and Carrie Neill of Adrian Smith + Gordon Gill Architecture, Chicago; Phil Enquist of Skidmore Owings and Merrill, Chicago (and Silas Chiow, SOM's representative in Shanghai); Robert Jacob and Scott Slaney of SWA Group, in Newport Beach, Calif., and Houston, respectively; and Brian Andrew and Robert Benjamin of WZMH, Toronto.

In Europe: Augusto Cagnardi of Gregotti Associati, Milan; Paul Andreu and Sabine Favre of Paul Andreu Architect, Paris; Jean-Marie Charpentier of Arte Charpentier, Paris; Johannes Dell of Albert Speer & Partner, Frankfurt; and Marcus Krotz, Tilke Architects, Aachen, Germany.

Thanks also to Dr. Christian Henriot, historian at the Stanford Humanities Center, for access to his Virtual Shanghai collection of vintage photography, and to Eric Politzer of Brooklyn, N.Y., for his knowledge and collection of antique and vintage images of Shanghai.

Special thanks to architect Bruce Halferty, his associate Chris Lin, and photographer Wang Da Gang, whose hospitality to me and my wife, Vanna Paoli, was boundless and whose deep knowledge of Shanghai was central to our understanding of this place and its architecture.

Also, editors Eric Himmel and Nancy Cohen deserve my unending thanks for their patience and commitment to making this the best book it could be.

JP

INDEX

Note: Page numbers in *italics* refer to illustrations and captions.

PHOTOGRAPH CREDITS

Editor: Nancy E. Cohen
Designer: Brady McNamara
Production Manager: Alison Gervais

Library of Congress Cataloging-in-Publication Data
Pridmore, Jay.
    Shanghai : the architecture of China's great urban center / by Jay
Pridmore.
        p. cm.
        ISBN-13: 978-0-8109-9406-5
        ISBN-10: 0-8109-9406-2
1. Architecture—China—Shanghai—20th century. 2. Architecture—China—
Shanghai—21st century. 3. Shanghai (China)—Buildings, structures, etc. I.
Title.
        NA1547.S5P75 2008
        720'.951132—dc22

                                                2007035142

Printed and bound in China
10 9 8 7 6 5 4 3 2 1

HNA
harry n. abrams, inc.
a subsidiary of La Martinière Groupe
115 West 18th Street
New York, NY 10011
www.hnabooks.com

Shanghai Pudong International Airport